NAKED
Mike Leigh

ff
faber and faber

First published in 1994 by
Faber and Faber Limited
3 Queen Square London WC1N 3AU

This edition published in 2000

Photoset by Parker Typesetting Service, Leicester
Printed and bound in England by
Mackays of Chatham plc, Chatham, Kent

A CIP record for this book is available from the British Library

ISBN 0-571-20264-0

2 4 6 8 10 9 7 5 3 1

CONTENTS

FOREWORD

I have often been asked whether I believe in the impending Apocalypse. Well, I do and I don't.

Will the world actually come to an abrupt end on 1st August 1999? Who can say? I think it's on the whole unlikely, myself.

But, like my despondent friend Johnny, I do worry about the future. We are, of course, destroying our total environment. Several thousand babies have been born since you started reading this page, but the planet has remained the same size. And we haven't learned to stop knocking lumps of each other.

So what sort of a world will my sons be living in when they're my age, circa 2030?

Should I be optimistic, and hope that things will somehow improve? Or is that unbearable recurring apocalyptic nightmare to be heeded?

Mike Leigh
London, October 1994

NAKED

Naked was first shown at the Cannes Film Festival on 14 May 1993. The cast and crew was as follows:

JOHNNY	David Thewlis
LOUISE	Lesley Sharp
SOPHIE	Katrin Cartlidge
JEREMY	Greg Cruttwell
SANDRA	Claire Skinner
BRIAN	Peter Wight
ARCHIE	Ewen Bremner
MAGGIE	Susan Vidler
WOMAN IN WINDOW	Deborah Maclaren
CAFÉ GIRL	Gina McKee
MASSEUSE	Carolina Giammetta
GISELLE	Elizabeth Berrington
POSTER MAN	Darren Tunstall
CHAUFFEUR	Robert Putt
VICTIM	Lynda Rooke
CAR OWNER	Angela Curran
MR HALPERN	Peter Whitman
WOMAN IN STREET	Jo Abercrombie
GIRL IN PORSCHE	Elaine Britten
TEA BAR OWNER	David Foxxe
MEN AT TEA BAR	Mike Avenall
	Toby Jones
BAG LADY	Sandra Voe

Written and directed by	Mike Leigh
Produced by	Simon Channing-Williams
Cinematographer	Dick Pope
Editor	Jon Gregory
Production Designer	Alison Chitty
Costume Designer	Lindy Hemming

Music   Andrew Dickson
Sound Recordist   Ken Weston

A Thin Man Film
for Film Four International
with the participation of British Screen.

Night. A dimly lit alley. The camera tracks rapidly towards a MAN
and a WOMAN *who are having a rough fuck under a streetlamp. They
are fully clothed.*

    At first, the WOMAN *seems enthusiastic.*

WOMAN: Oh! Oh! Oh! Go on! Oh! Oh! O-ooh! Oh, oh, ooh! Oh!
    Oh! (*Then, suddenly*) Ow!! Shit! What're you do –? Ow!!
    (*He is pushing her head back, his hand under her chin. His other
    hand pins down her wrist.*)
    You're hurting me –!
    (*Now crying, she tries to push him off. After a brief struggle, he
    releases her and she breaks free.
    She runs a few paces and turns round. He has his back to her. He
    is fixing his trousers.*)

WOMAN: (*Shouting*) I'm gonna tell my Bernard of you!! You're
    fuckin' dead!!
    (*She runs off into the night, and so does he – in the opposite
    direction.*)

A short time later, the MAN *rushes out of a terraced house, clutching a
canvas shoulder-bag. He races along the street and round a corner.*

    *Moments after this, he is running down another alley, past the backs
of houses.*

    *An old saloon car is standing with its boot open. He stops. The
ignition key is in the boot-lock. A baby-buggy is sticking out of the boot
itself. He pushes this inside, grabs the keys and slams down the lid.*

    *The offside car doors are open. He shuts the rear, throws his bag on
to the passenger seat, jumps in, starts the engine and drives off at great
speed, closing his door as he goes.*

    A small, irate WOMAN *runs out of the nearest house. She shouts
after the car as it disappears.*

WOMAN: Oi!! Come back 'ere, you!! Ronnie! Geroff that couch
    and come out 'ere!! (*She races into her back yard.*) Ronnie!

All night, the MAN *drives the stolen car down almost empty night-time
motorways.*

Early morning, central London. Office blocks, the Telecom Tower in the distance. The car pulls off an urban clearway and skids to a halt. The MAN *jumps out with his bag and runs off, abandoning the car with its engine running.*

Later in the day. An old inner-city residential district. Surrounded by decaying houses, JOHNNY *(for that is his name) is standing in the middle of the road. He is holding a piece of paper. He looks lost.*

Shortly after this, JOHNNY *is sitting on a low wall at the top of the long flight of steps leading up to the front door of a large Victorian Neo-Gothic house.*

SOPHIE *ambles towards the house. She climbs the steps. At the top . . .*

SOPHIE: Oh, shit – sorry! I didn't see you there.

JOHNNY: Do you live 'ere?

SOPHIE: Yeah . . . I do, unfortunately.

JOHNNY: Do you know Louise Clancy?

SOPHIE: Yeah. Are you a friend of 'ers?

JOHNNY: Know where she is?

SOPHIE: She's at work.

JOHNNY: What time does she get back?

SOPHIE: Dunno. About seven or something.

JOHNNY: Fuckin' hell!

(*Pause.*)

SOPHIE: D'you wanna come in for a cuppa tea?

JOHNNY: Is that all right with you, love? It's just . . . you know . . . cold.

Moments later, inside. JOHNNY *is following* SOPHIE *up the stairs of the flat.*

JOHNNY: Listen, have you got anything for a headache?

SOPHIE: Ah . . . yeah, we 'ave as it 'appens.

JOHNNY: You know, like a monkey-wrench or somethin'.

(SOPHIE *laughs, and opens the bathroom door.* JOHNNY *stops at a wall-diagram of the human skeleton.*)

What's all this about?

SOPHIE: Oh, yeah . . . that's Sandra, that is.

JOHNNY: Hallo, Sandra!

6

(SOPHIE *laughs*.)

SOPHIE: This is 'er place. She's a fuckin' nurse. That's 'er idea of interior design.

JOHNNY: Oh, yeah – it's a skeleton.

(*She opens a large medicine chest.*)

SOPHIE: And this is 'er cocktail cabinet, an' all. (*She takes out a pill bottle.*) There you go . . . that should do it.

(*She gives him the bottle. He puts it in his mouth.*)

JOHNNY: No, it's too big.

(*She laughs and walks away. He returns his attention to the skeleton.*)

SOPHIE: D'you want a cuppa tea?

JOHNNY: Yeah.

A few minutes have passed. SOPHIE *is standing in the middle of her kitchen.* JOHNNY *is leaning against a cupboard. He pops a headache pill into his mouth.*

SOPHIE: So, are you Louise's boyfriend?

JOHNNY: No.

SOPHIE: Oh, right. What, you're just like a mate?

JOHNNY: Primate. (*He takes his bag off his shoulder and drops it on the floor.*)

SOPHIE: You must be the missing link, then?

JOHNNY: Yeah, that's me.

SOPHIE: You're not gonna tell me your name?

JOHNNY: No.

SOPHIE: I'm not gonna tell you mine neither.

JOHNNY: All right . . . We'll be strangers.

A little while later, in the living room. Close-up of a boomerang, sitting amongst other assorted ethnic artefacts on a shelf.

JOHNNY: I see your boomerang came back then, love.

SOPHIE: It's not my fuckin' boomerang.

(*The camera tilts to a set of ebony elephants on the shelf below.*)

JOHNNY: What about the old diminishing pachyderm formation there?

SOPHIE: No, that's all Sandra's collection. She's in Zimbabwe at the moment. And fuck knows what she's gonna bring back from there.

7

(SOPHIE *is sitting on a floor cushion. She passes a joint to* JOHNNY, *who is sitting close by in an armchair.*)

JOHNNY: Pellagra or hepatitis B or something.

SOPHIE: She's with her boyfriend.

(SOPHIE *pulls down her already skimpy garment to reveal bare shoulders, throwing* JOHNNY *a moody glance as she does so. Pause.*)

JOHNNY: So, how is Louise?

SOPHIE: I dunno . . . I don't know 'er as well as you.

JOHNNY: D'you get on with 'er?

SOPHIE: We've been out a couple o' times.

JOHNNY: Does she like you?

SOPHIE: I dunno – you'd better ask 'er. Most people don't.

JOHNNY: D'you find that she's at all jealous of you?

SOPHIE: No.

JOHNNY: So . . . I dunno . . . Would you describe yourself as a . . . happy little person?

SOPHIE: Yeah . . . I'm the life and soul.

JOHNNY: Have you ever thought, right . . . I mean, you don't know, but you might already 'ave had the happiest moment in your whole fuckin' life, and all you've got to look forward to is sickness and purgatory?

SOPHIE: Oh, shit! Well . . . I just live from day to day, meself. (*She takes back the joint.*)

JOHNNY: I tend to skip a day now and again – you know what I mean? I used to be a werewolf, but I'm all right NOW!!

SOPHIE: Oh, fuckin' 'ell!! I bet they're 'appy, eh? All they gotta do is sit round, howlin' at the moon.

JOHNNY: It's better than standin' on the cheesy fuckin' thing. Know what I mean? I mean, tossin' all these satellites and shuttles out into the cosmos – what do they think they're gonna find up there that they can't find down 'ere? They think if they piss high enough, they're gonna come across the monkey with the beard and the crap ideas, and it's like, 'Oh, there you are, Captain! I mean . . . are you busy, because I've got a few fundamental questions for you!' Are you with me?

SOPHIE: Yeah . . . 'cos let's face it, right, what are rockets? I mean, they're just . . . big metal pricks! You know, I mean,

9

the bastards aren't satisfied with fuckin' the earth up –
they've gotta fuck space an' all.

(JOHNNY *takes back the joint*.)

JOHNNY: Will you tell me something, love? Are you aware of the
effect you have on the average mammalian, Mancunian,
x-y-ly-chromosome, slavering, lusty male member of the
species?

SOPHIE: Er . . . yeah.

JOHNNY: I thought so.

Meanwhile, in a busy state-of-the-art gym, JEREMY *is exercising his
arm muscles on an elaborate machine. He is working very hard.
Behind him, a row of men sweat it out on running machines.*

*Later, he is in the massage room on the bed, lying on his back. He is
wearing nothing but a small towel over his private parts. The*
MASSEUSE *is doing his leg.*

JEREMY: Would you like to have dinner with me tonight?

MASSEUSE: No!

(*A few minutes later, she is massaging his chest.*)

JEREMY: Do you think women like being raped?

(*Now* JEREMY *has turned over on to his tummy.*)

MASSEUSE: You talk a lot, don't you?

JEREMY: Do you like Japanese food?

MASSEUSE: Look, I've told you – I'm not interested. All right?
(*She is pummelling his back.*)

JEREMY: Could I have that a touch harder, please?

MASSEUSE: Yes! (*She pummels his back very hard indeed.*)

The same day, early evening. LOUISE *comes through the front door of the flat and walks up the stairs. She is chewing gum. On the landing she hears* SOPHIE *laughing. The living-room door is open. She goes in.*

LOUISE: All right? Enjoyin' yourself, are you?
(*She puts her keys away.* SOPHIE *is sitting in an armchair.*)

SOPHIE: I'm 'avin' a great time, actually.
(SOPHIE *giggles. So does the voice of* JOHNNY – *he isn't visible.* LOUISE *looks round in surprise and advances towards the sofa. She sees him peeping at her.*)

LOUISE: Bloody 'ell!

JOHNNY: Oh, friendly!

LOUISE: What are you doin' 'ere? You look like shit.

JOHNNY: Just tryin' to blend in with the surroundings.
(LOUISE *leans over and kisses him.*)

JOHNNY: (*Sings, to the tune of Handel's 'Hallelujah!'*) Halitosis! Halitosis, Halitosis!
(SOPHIE *giggles.* JOHNNY *sits up.*)

LOUISE: I can't believe you're 'ere.

JOHNNY: I'm not 'ere. I tell you what, it's a crackin' place you got, love.

LOUISE: Good. I'm glad you like it.

JOHNNY: No, I was being sarcastic.

LOUISE: Why didn't you tell me you were comin'? I would a' met you off the train.

JOHNNY: I didn't come on the fuckin' train.

LOUISE: Off the bus, then.

JOHNNY: I didn't come on a bus either.

LOUISE: So 'ow did you get 'ere, then?

JOHNNY: Well, basically . . . There was this little dot, right? And the dot went bang, and the bang expanded, energy formed into matter, matter cooled, matter lived, the amoeba the fish, the fish the fowl, the fowl the froggy, the froggy the mammal, the mammal the monkey, the monkey the man.

Amo, amas, amat, quid pro quo, memento mori, ad infinitum,
sprinkle on a little bit of grated cheese and leave under the
grill till Doomsday.

(*Much giggling from* SOPHIE. LOUISE *has sat down.*)

LOUISE: See you 'aven't changed.

SOPHIE: 'E's a fuckin' genius, this geezer!

LOUISE: I take it you've met my wicky-wacky friend Sophie?

JOHNNY: No, actually . . . we 'aven't been formally introduced,
  'ave we, love?

SOPHIE: No.

JOHNNY: No, we've been sat 'ere in embarrassin' silence all
  afternoon. (*Pause.*) So . . . 'ow are you?

LOUISE: Peachy-creamy.

  (SOPHIE *giggles.*)

JOHNNY: Are you really? I'm very pleased. So how's, um . . .
  work?

LOUISE: It's all right.

JOHNNY: It's all right.

LOUISE: It's all right.

JOHNNY: Is it everything you hoped it would be?

LOUISE: Yeah.

JOHNNY: What did you hope it would be?

  (*Pause.* LOUISE *exhales some cigarette smoke.*)
  I'm sorry – did you get that? It's everything she hoped it
  would be, but she doesn't fuckin' know what she hoped it
  would be! Oh, and by the way . . . Thank you . . . for this!
  (*He takes out a crumpled postcard.*) I mean, are you tekkin' the
  piss, or what? (*Reads.*) 'So, Johnny . . . My address is . . .'
  (*Mock snore.* SOPHIE *giggles.*)
  I'm touched.
  (*Pause.*)

LOUISE: Why 'ave you come?

JOHNNY: Oh, can you tell from there?

  (*Pause.* SOPHIE *giggles.*)

LOUISE: D'you want a cup o' tea?

JOHNNY: I'd love a cup o' tea. You're fuckin' generous, you
  cockerneys, aren't yer?

LOUISE: (*Getting up*) Sophie?

SOPHIE: Er, yeah. Ta.

(LOUISE *stops for a moment in the doorway and looks at the other
two, then goes out.*
JOHNNY *turns to* SOPHIE, *who is looking at him very intensely.
In the cluttered kitchen,* LOUISE *drops a teabag into each of three
mugs. Then she picks up the postcard, looks at it, tears it in half
and throws it into an overflowing rubbish bin.*)

*A few minutes later, all three are in the living room with their tea.
Johnny is smoking a cigarette, Sophie a joint.* JOHNNY *is still sitting
on the sofa.* LOUISE *squats on its arm.* SOPHIE *is standing.*

JOHNNY: 'Ow's yer mam?

LOUISE: Fine. 'Ow's yours? Still pullin' pints?

JOHNNY: She's dead. She's still a good fuck, though. I mean, the
    rates are a bit extortionate, but I do get a discount, what with
    being the son and everything.

SOPHIE: Apparently, right, you shouldn't stick anything up your
    cunt that you can't put in your mouth.

JOHNNY: (*To* LOUISE) Give us that mug!
    (SOPHIE *giggles.*)

SOPHIE: Can I try your coat on, Johnny?

JOHNNY: Yeah.
    (*She proceeds to do so.*)

LOUISE: So, what've you been up to? 'Ave you seen anybody?

JOHNNY: Have you seen anybody? Have you spoken to anybody
    from Manchester?

LOUISE: Yeah, I phoned June a couple o' times.

JOHNNY: And was June interested in what you had to say?
    (SOPHIE *sits down in an armchair. Pause.*)
    Fuckin' hell! I've seen more life in an open grave. Come on!!

LOUISE: What?

JOHNNY: What?! I mean, you don't seem very pleased to see me.

LOUISE: I am pleased to see you!

JOHNNY: Are you too good for us? Now you've got yourself a
    posh job in the big 'shitty'? I mean, me an' 'er are on the
    fuckin' dole, aren't we?

SOPHIE: Right!

JOHNNY: And you're a career girl – are you happy with that?

LOUISE: Yeah.

JOHNNY: Are you sure?

14

LOUISE: Yeah.

JOHNNY: I'm delighted.

(*Pause.*)

SOPHIE: D'you want some o' this, Johnny? (*She leans forward with the joint.*)

JOHNNY: Fuckin' 'ell, love . . . What're you tryin' to do to me? (*He takes the joint. Pause.*)

LOUISE: (*Getting up*) Right, well, I'm going up to me room. D'you wanna see it, Johnny?

JOHNNY: Is it worth the bother? Is there anything worth seein'?

LOUISE: Why don't you come and find out? It's not very far. (*She goes out.* SOPHIE *giggles.* JOHNNY *now has both the cigarette and the joint in his mouth. He grimaces and takes them both out.*)

JOHNNY: I'm sorry about this. (*He gets up and goes out, carrying his mug of tea, the cigarette, the joint and his tobacco tin. He climbs the stairs with some effort and comes to a halt near the top.*) Move! Move! (*He drops back down a few steps and stops with his back to the wall. He emits an exasperated snort, then, after a moment and with some effort, he continues the journey upstairs.*) Where are you?

LOUISE: (*From her room*) I'm in 'ere.

(*He appears in her doorway.*)

JOHNNY: Oh! It's de-lovely! I see you've got a ceiling at the top with a floor on the lower level, and a wall at either side. And only a single bed. Sad, really . . .

(*He leaves. She is sitting on her bed by the window. Her curtains are open. Cars bustle by in the night-time street below.*)

Meanwhile, in a candle-lit posh restaurant, JEREMY *is entertaining the* MASSEUSE *to dinner. She is wearing an extremely low-cut dress. A* WAITRESS *is standing close by, opening a bottle of champagne. She is also scantily clad.*

JEREMY: You've got wonderful breasts.

MASSEUSE: Don't you mean tits?

JEREMY: Are they both the same size, or is one bigger than the other?

MASSEUSE: I don't know. D'you want to weigh them? (*The* WAITRESS *pops the cork.*)

JEREMY: Is that a proposition?

MASSEUSE: No, it's a threat.

(*A little later,* JEREMY *is consuming a small bird. He tears off its wings, picks up its carcass in his bare hands and attacks it hungrily. The* MASSEUSE *watches.*)

Are you rich?

JEREMY: Life is for enjoying. (*He doesn't look at her.*)

MASSEUSE: What about family, have you got any brothers or sisters?

JEREMY: I try not to remember.

MASSEUSE: You're sexually frustrated, aren't you?

(JEREMY *looks at her, then sniggers.*)

What's funny?

JEREMY: Are you a feminist?

MASSEUSE: No.

JEREMY: Do you like fucking?

MASSEUSE: Do you like wanking?

JEREMY: Not on my own, no.

(*She looks away. His eyes stay on her as he licks his sticky fingers.*)

Back at the flat, JOHNNY *is studying the bird tattoo on Sophie's left shoulder.*

JOHNNY: That's a very ornithological mutilation you've got there, love. (*He kisses the tattoo gently.*)

SOPHIE: That's my tribal initiation.

JOHNNY: Is it really?

(*He pulls her towards him. They embrace and kiss warmly. Together they fall clumsily on to the sofa.* SOPHIE *giggles.*)

SOPHIE: That was fuckin' athletic, that was.

JOHNNY: I think I've ruptured my chakras.

(*A few minutes later,* SOPHIE *is kneeling astride* JOHNNY, *who is facing her. He is embarking on trying to unlace her leather bodice.*)

Is there an instruction manual for this garb?

SOPHIE: No . . . It's an intelligence test.

JOHNNY: Now what is this? A granny, a sheepshank, or the infamous round-turn and two half-hitches, as mentioned in the Book of Ezekiel?

SOPHIE: Have you finished?

JOHNNY: I've hardly fuckin' begun. It's just that I think I'm gonna get into difficulties when I read the hippy-shit up here, you know what I mean? (*He fiddles with some tassels at the top of the bodice.*)

SOPHIE: Yeah . . . Well, you've tried the stairs. I think we should take the escalator. (*She swivels the bodice round and undoes its side zip.*) Simple, really. So's this.

(*She takes his hand and places it inside her top.*)

JOHNNY: Oh. Thanks for the mammaries.

At the restaurant, the WAITRESS *is serving the coffee.*

MASSEUSE: Could you ask her to order me a taxi, please?

JEREMY: This is terribly disappointing.

MASSEUSE: You don't like rejection, do you, Jeremy?

JEREMY: Could we have a taxi, please?

WAITRESS: No problem . . . sir.

(*The* WAITRESS *walks away.* JEREMY *watches her go.*)

Meanwhile, JOHNNY *and* SOPHIE *lie on the sofa, stripped to the waist. They kiss passionately, with a hint of sexual aggression, which is mutual, though initiated by* JOHNNY.

Following SOPHIE *up the stairs,* JOHNNY *gives her a playful smack on the bottom. (They are both still wearing their black jeans.) Then they kiss briefly. No sexual aggression from* JOHNNY. SOPHIE *proceeds upstairs.* JOHNNY *stays for a moment, leaning against the wall. He is tense.*

In Sophie's room. They are making love on the floor. SOPHIE *is on top. It is passionate and loving. No aggression from* JOHNNY. *Ecstatic moans from* SOPHIE.

Whilst in the next room, LOUISE *is lying on her bed, wide awake, smoking. Her curtains and her windows are still open. Below, street lamps mingle with the twinkling headlights of passing cars.*

Later, SOPHIE *lies asleep on her bed.* JOHNNY *sits next to her, leaning against the wall, awake, still naked. He holds his chest. He gets up and leaves the room.*

Whilst all this has been going on, JEREMY *has taken the* WAITRESS *from the restaurant back to his cold, trendy bachelor flat, with its polished wooden floor and its harsh black-and-white décor.*

And now, in the middle of the night, JEREMY *is sprawling on his leather sofa, holding a champagne bottle and a glass.*

At the other end of the room, the WAITRESS, *also holding a glass, does the splits.*

WAITRESS: Wheeee!!

> (*She lands on her back on the hard floor and has a burst of the giggles. Then, still giggling and making 'wheee' sounds, she crawls on all fours across the floor and flops on to the sofa beside* JEREMY.
>
> *For a while, he doesn't look at her or move.*)

WAITRESS: It's really cosy, this. (*Pause.*) Will you let me come again, Jerry? (*Pause.*) You're dead handsome, you know. (*Pause. She strokes his hair. He doesn't respond.*) What work d'you do? (*Pause.*) I'm a dancer, actually. (*Pause.*) Don't you want to know me name? It's Giselle. (*Pause.*) Are you married?

> (JEREMY *looks at her.*)
>
> (*Bemused*) Wha'?

JEREMY: Kiss me.

> (*She does so, with great feeling. After a few moments, she screams with pain and sits back.* JEREMY *sniggers. She manages to smile bravely and nurses her lip.*)
>
> (*A little later.* JEREMY *is still on the sofa.* GISELLE *is kneeling on the floor, facing him. He is rubbing a stuffed lizard up her bare arm. [She is still wearing her sleeveless, low-cut garment.*])

GISELLE: Don't . . . it's yucky! Get it off!

> (*She giggles. He makes the lizard 'bite' her left breast.*)
>
> Are you glad I came?
>
> (*Suddenly and violently, he makes the lizard go for her neck.*)
>
> What are you doin'? Get off me!!

In JEREMY'S *bedroom. He throws* GISELLE *roughly on to the bed and kneels over her, grasping her wrists and pinning them down.*

> You're hurting me!

JEREMY: Have you ever thought of committing suicide?

GISELLE: No.

JEREMY: I'm going to commit suicide. On my fortieth birthday. If I'm still around.

GISELLE: (*Crying*) Why?

JEREMY: I don't want to be old. Do you?
> (*He falls violently on her neck. She screams out loud in pain and fear.*)

Very early next morning. Cold, grey daylight. Louise's curtains flap in the wind. She wakes suddenly, as from a nightmare, and sits up. She shuts her window and pulls the duvet round her. She is shivering. She listens for a sound.

Downstairs, in the living room, a little later. JOHNNY *is sitting in an armchair, reading a book (James Gleick: Chaos). He is wearing only his overcoat and he is smoking.* LOUISE *hands him a mug of tea. He takes it without looking at her. She sits on the sofa and takes one of his cigarettes.*

JOHNNY: Oh. 'Ave a fag.
LOUISE: Yeah. Thanks. I will. (*She lights it and settles back on the sofa.*) What're you readin'? (*Pause. She picks up Sophie's bodice and examines it.*)
JOHNNY: Will you stop fuckin' about and fidgetin' in my peripherals – I'm tryin' to concentrate.
> (LOUISE *is holding the bodice in front of her face.*)

LOUISE: She's got a very little waist, Sophie, an't she? (*She peeps at him over the top of the bodice.*) She's got little tits an' all. (*She throws down the bodice.*) Are you not cold?
JOHNNY: I'm readin' about the Butterfly Effect.
LOUISE: What's the Butterfly Effect?
JOHNNY: Every time a butterfly flaps its wings in Tokyo, this old granny in Salford gets a bilious attack.
LOUISE: What happens if a butterfly flaps its wings in Salford?
JOHNNY: That's not the point.
LOUISE: Oh, is it not? What are you doin' in London, Johnny?
JOHNNY: What are you doin' in London?
LOUISE: I've told you what I'm doin' in London.
JOHNNY: You've told me nothing.
LOUISE: The last time I saw you, I told you –
> (*He throws down the book.*)

JOHNNY: Fuckin' hell! Were you born irritatin'? What have you come downstairs for anyway?
LOUISE: I fell asleep with the window open. I was cold. I came down. I 'ad a pee. I've made some tea. I'm 'ere. All right?

JOHNNY: What's that? The greatest story ever told?

LOUISE: I live 'ere. (*Pause.*) So what 'appened? Were you bored in Manchester?

JOHNNY: Was I bored? No, I wasn't fuckin' bored. I'm never bored. That's the trouble with everybody – you're all so bored. You've 'ad nature explained to you and you're bored with it. You've 'ad the living body explained to you and you're bored with it. You've 'ad the universe explained to you and you're bored with it. So now you just want cheap thrills and like plenty of 'em, and it dun't matter 'ow tawdry or vacuous they are as long as it's new, as long as it's new, as long as it flashes and fuckin' bleeps in forty fuckin' different colours. Well, whatever else you can say about me, I'm not fuckin' bored!

LOUISE: Yeah, all right.

JOHNNY: So, 'ow's it goin' for you?

LOUISE: It's a bit borin', actually.

JOHNNY: Are you not enjoyin' yourself?

(LOUISE *shakes her head.*)

Have you made many friends?

LOUISE: No.

JOHNNY: 'Ave you got, erm, a goblet or something, because me heart's bleedin'.

LOUISE: When are you goin' back to Manchester?

JOHNNY: When are *you* goin' back to Manchester?

LOUISE: I'm not going back.

JOHNNY: Why not?

LOUISE: You know why not.

JOHNNY: Do I?

LOUISE: I thought you said you never wanted to see me again.

JOHNNY: I don't ever wanna see you again, so will you fuck off back upstairs?

LOUISE: Why are you such a bastard, Johnny?

(JOHNNY *coughs.*)

JOHNNY: Monkey see, monkey do.

LOUISE: And what does that mean?

(JOHNNY *has a short bout of coughing.*)

JOHNNY: Oh, this fuckin' cough.

LOUISE: Mm. A butterfly must 'ave flapped its wings.

(*He coughs again.*)

JOHNNY: So, have you got to get up for work now, yeah?
LOUISE: No. It's too early. I'm going back to bed.
(*He coughs.* LOUISE *gets up and leaves the room. His cough continues.*)

Later. Broad daylight. A small, fat Buddha sits on a low table, surrounded by joss sticks, beads and bells. We are in Sandra's tasteful bedroom. JOHNNY *squats before this shrine.*
JOHNNY: So is she a – a Buddhist or something, this nurse?
(SOPHIE *walks past him.*)
SOPHIE: No. She's a Catholic.
JOHNNY: What's she doin' with the old fat chap in the house, then?
(*He turns his attention to some books.*)
SOPHIE: Dunno. I think she fancies him or somethin'.
(JOHNNY *takes out a large volume of anatomy.*)
JOHNNY: Louise is a Catholic. Did you know that?
SOPHIE: She's not, is she?
(JOHNNY *opens the book at a diagram.*)
JOHNNY: Oh, fuckin' hell!
(*Pause.* SOPHIE *wanders over to a blue nurse's uniform, which is hanging from a dormer window. She holds it against herself for a moment.*)
You know what frightens me about the human body?
(SOPHIE *hangs up the uniform.*)
SOPHIE: What?
JOHNNY: Well, it's like the, er, most sophisticated mechanism in the entire universe, and yet it's so fucking quiet, in't it? Know what I mean?
SOPHIE: Dunno . . . Mine makes enough noise.
(*She lies on the double bed.* JOHNNY *sits next to her, on the edge of the bed, holding the open anatomy.*)
JOHNNY: It's like this, er, wet, pink factory. What the fuck are they makin' in there? I mean, what's the product? You never see no delivery trucks comin' or goin', do you? (*He browses through the book.*) I could've been a doctor.
SOPHIE: D'you wanna examine me?
JOHNNY: You don't believe me, do you?
SOPHIE: I believe everythink you say.
JOHNNY: I've got A-level Psychology.

22

SOPHIE: You 'aven't!

JOHNNY: 'Resolve is never stronger than in the morning after the
    night it was never weaker.' What d'you think of that?

SOPHIE: It's a load of bollocks. (*She giggles.*)

JOHNNY: I thought of that. D'you not agree with it?

SOPHIE: Dunno . . .

JOHNNY: Yeah, well, that's 'cos you weren't fuckin' listening,
    were you?

    (SOPHIE *sits up.*)

SOPHIE: What's this? A test or somethin'?

    (*She fondles Johnny's hair. They kiss, gently.*)

Shortly after this, JOHNNY *and* SOPHIE *are walking along a busy high
street. People. Shops. Traffic.*

    SOPHIE *playfully head-butts* JOHNNY *in the small of his back.*

JOHNNY: Don't! Stop it!

    (SOPHIE *giggles.*)

    Just pack it in! Stop it!

    (SOPHIE *swings on a lamppost.*)

    Stop buggering about!

    (JOHNNY *keeps on walking.* SOPHIE *catches up with him,
    dancing about with merry abandon.*)

SOPHIE: You could get me a watch, Johnny . . .

JOHNNY: Will you just keep still?!

    (*They pass a watch-stall.*)

SOPHIE: Look, you could get me a watch . . .

JOHNNY: I'm not gonna get you a watch – you don't want a fuckin'
    watch!!

    (*They proceed through the crowds.*)

Back at the flat, towards the end of the afternoon. It is still light. SOPHIE *is
kneeling astride* JOHNNY, *stroking him. They are both fully clothed.*

SOPHIE: I really like you, Johnny.

JOHNNY: You don't know me. (*He strokes her hair.*)

SOPHIE: I think I do.

JOHNNY: You don't fuckin' – (*He pulls her abruptly down to him by
    the hair.*)

SOPHIE: Oh, shit!

JOHNNY: – know me!

SOPHIE: Fuckin' hell!

    (*He pins her arm behind her back.*)

JOHNNY: D'you still like me?

SOPHIE: I love you.

JOHNNY: What?

SOPHIE: I'm in love with you, Johnny.

    (*He laughs.*)

    Don't laugh – I'm serious, uh!

    (*Grasping her hair very tightly, he forces her head upwards, then
    down into his chest. She gasps for breath.*)

    I understand you, Johnny . . . I do.

*Minutes later, still fully clothed, they are having a fuck at the other end
of the sofa.* JOHNNY *is on top. He is holding Sophie's face roughly. She
gasps and whimpers and struggles. He starts to bang her head against
the arm of the sofa.*

SOPHIE: Oh! Oh! Oh! Oh! Oh! Johnn– . . . No, no, . . . Johnny!
    Oh! Oh! Oh! . . .

Meanwhile, LOUISE *is standing at a filing cabinet in the office where
she works. A small, neat middle-aged man, wearing a hat and coat,
rushes past her.*

LOUISE: Ta-ra, Mr Halpern.

    (MR HALPERN *rushes back and disappears whence he came.*
    LOUISE *continues to file documents. A moment later,* MR
    HALPERN *rushes past her again, bearing a bunch of flowers.*
    LOUISE *glances after him unlovingly and returns her attention to a
    piece of paper.*)

The same evening. In the living room. SOPHIE *lounges on the sofa.*
JOHNNY *sits in an armchair, reading a book. Suddenly, he gets up and
goes into the kitchen.* SOPHIE *follows.* LOUISE *is just leaving with a
mug and a piece of toast.* SOPHIE *moves to* JOHNNY.

SOPHIE: What's the matter? What's goin' on?

JOHNNY: Fucked if I know.

    (*He goes back into the living room.* SOPHIE *follows.* LOUISE *has
    put on the television and is sitting on the sofa.* JOHNNY *leans on the
    sofa with his back to* LOUISE. *Pause. The TV programme
    concerns horses.*)

24

I'm too old for all this.

(*He returns to the kitchen.* SOPHIE *follows and leans in the kitchen doorway.*)

SOPHIE: Why don't we go out? Go for a drink or somethin'?

JOHNNY: Why don't you go out – go for a drink or somethin'?

(*He goes back into the living room.* SOPHIE *follows.*)

SOPHIE: 'Cos I wanna go with you!

(*He stops by the television.* [*Horses outside Buckingham Palace.*])

JOHNNY: Er, is this good?

(*He turns it off.* LOUISE *gets up and turns it back on. He returns to the kitchen.* SOPHIE *follows.*)

SOPHIE: What are you doin'?

(*He picks up his coat from the kitchen floor and puts it on.*)
Where are you goin'?

JOHNNY: I'm cold!

SOPHIE: Johnny, I just –

(*She tries to snuggle up to him. He pushes her away.*)

JOHNNY: Fuck off!

(*He goes back into the living room.* SOPHIE *follows. As he enters, he turns round and goes and sits half-way up the stairs.* SOPHIE *follows, and hangs on the banister rail near him.*)

JOHNNY: Fuckin' hell! D'you ever get the feelin' that you're bein' followed? Look, will you just leave me alone – give me a bit of room or something'?

(SOPHIE *clears off.* JOHNNY *writhes for a few moments. Then he goes back into the living room.* SOPHIE *is leaning by the wall.* JOHNNY *stands in front of* LOUISE. *He takes her cigarette, has a drag, flicks the ash on the floor, and bends down and kisses* LOUISE *on the lips.* SOPHIE *turns away and thumps the wall.*)

SOPHIE: Fuckin' hell!

(*The kiss over,* JOHNNY *returns to the kitchen.* SOPHIE *rushes after him.*)
Johnny! Johnny!

(*He is putting his canvas bag on his shoulder.*)
What's all that about? What are you playin' at?

(*He kisses her. She responds passionately. Then he makes off down the stairs. She clings on to him.*)

26

Where are you goin', Johnny?

JOHNNY: Er, off my head.

(*He breaks free and continues downstairs. She follows.*)

SOPHIE: I'm comin' with you.

JOHNNY: No, you're not.

SOPHIE: I wanna come with you!

(*He throws her down on the stairs.*)

JOHNNY: I don't want you to fucking come with me! (*He disappears towards the front door.*)

SOPHIE: (*Shouting*) Are you coming back?

JOHNNY: (*From below*) What the fuck for?

(*Outside.* JOHNNY *slams the front door and rushes down the steps and across the empty street into the cold night.*)

Later that night. JOHNNY *saunters aimlessly along a crowded West End street. And then along a rather emptier street, where he stops by a closed shop on a corner. He puts down his bag and sits on the step.*

A youth with no topcoat is hovering restlessly.

YOUNG MAN: (*Shouting*) Maggie! Maggie!

(*This person is called Archie, which* JOHNNY *will discover later.* JOHNNY *takes out a cigarette and lights it. Cars pass.*)

JOHNNY: You all right there, chief? 'Ave you lost somebody?

ARCHIE: Eh?

JOHNNY: Are you lookin' for somebody?

ARCHIE: Fuck off, cunt!!

(*Pause. A man walks past one way, a taxi drives by the other.* ARCHIE *goes and stands over* JOHNNY.)

Got a fag?

JOHNNY: Yes, thanks.

ARCHIE: Uh?

JOHNNY: Yeah, I got one.

ARCHIE: Giz one.

JOHNNY: Please.

ARCHIE: Wha'?

JOHNNY: Say please.

ARCHIE: Just fuckin' giz one. Come on, mister!

JOHNNY: You've got a lovely way about you – 'as anybody ever told you that?

(*He gives* ARCHIE *a cigarette.* ARCHIE *walks away.*)

'Thank you!' 'That's all right.'

(*Throughout this scene, cars and people pass by intermittently.*)

ARCHIE: Maggie!

JOHNNY: She's gone, mate!

ARCHIE: Eh?

JOHNNY: (*Slight laugh*) Those days are over.

ARCHIE: Have you seen a lassie wanderin' aboot here?

JOHNNY: What?

ARCHIE: A lassie. Black hair, blue jeans.

JOHNNY: I saw a little Border collie padding off down there towards the fire.

ARCHIE: Where?

JOHNNY: 'Ave you lost your bird or somethin'?

ARCHIE: Aye. Have you seen her? Black hair?

JOHNNY: No.

ARCHIE: Fuckin' 'ell! Stupid fuckin' cunt's gone and got lost. (*He sits next to* JOHNNY.)

JOHNNY: Are you from Scotland?

ARCHIE: Uh?

JOHNNY: Are you Scots?

ARCHIE: Aye.

JOHNNY: What's it like up there?

ARCHIE: Fuckin' shite! I'll kick her fanny in.

JOHNNY: D'you dream in Scotch?

ARCHIE: Uh?

JOHNNY: Like, dream about sporran-clad, caber-tossin' haggis, gallopin' over porridge-covered glens?

ARCHIE: Talking shite.

JOHNNY: Yeah, well, I sent off for one of those little Linguaphone packages, 'Talk Shite in a Fortnight' – 't's all goin' very well. I haven't quite got the hang of the transitive verbs yet, but –

ARCHIE: Will you fuckin' shut it, eh?! (*He coughs.*)

A little later, JOHNNY *and* ARCHIE *are walking along a main West End shopping street. Brightly lit window displays. A police siren somewhere nearby.* ARCHIE *twitches, a slight toss of the head.*

JOHNNY: So, what are you doin' down 'ere?

ARCHIE: Eh?

JOHNNY: Why are you here in London, O Bodhidharma?

ARCHIE: Put my old man in hospital.

JOHNNY: Your dad?

ARCHIE: Ah. (*Another twitch*)

JOHNNY: 'Ow did you do that, then?

ARCHIE: Cracked 'im on the nut wi' a poker. (*Another twitch. These happen frequently.*)

JOHNNY: What for?

ARCHIE: 'E was fuckin' askin' for it! (*Shouting*) Maggie!!!

JOHNNY: So what, is 'e in a bad way?

ARCHIE: Fuckin' right. He's 'alf dead.

JOHNNY: What does your mam think about it?

ARCHIE: She's off 'er fuckin' nut.

JOHNNY: So you're like on the run, yeah?

ARCHIE: Aye.

JOHNNY: Yeah, me too.

ARCHIE: Yeah? The cops after you? Yeah?

    (*A little further on, they stop outside a closed bar between two lit neon signs ('Bar' and 'Bar').*)

JOHNNY: Can you tell me somethin', Jock.

ARCHIE: (*Twitching*) Uh?

JOHNNY: What's all that about? (*He imitates the twitch.*)

ARCHIE: Eh?

JOHNNY: That. The old . . . Highland fling, there. D'you know why you're doin' that?

ARCHIE: What?

JOHNNY: That, you know – 'And for my next tic . . .' That.

(ARCHIE *does it.*)

Look, it, it just happened again – I'm not imaginin' it.

ARCHIE: Fuck off, eh?

JOHNNY: D'you do that in the sack with the old tic, spit, 'Eh, Maggie!'? Must be a great fuckin' shag!

ARCHIE: Are you takin' the piss?

JOHNNY: You're fuckin' givin' it away, aren't yer?

(ARCHIE *squares up close to* JOHNNY.)

ARCHIE: Fuckin' come on, cunt! Kick your fuckin' head open!! Eh?

JOHNNY: What's it like bein' you?

ARCHIE: Eh?

JOHNNY: Bit 'ectic?

ARCHIE: Fuck off, poof!

(ARCHIE *leaves.* JOHNNY *follows.*)

Minutes later. They have returned to the corner shop. The street has got busier. Neon lights flash in the distance.

JOHNNY: Do you believe in self-fulfillin' prophecy?

ARCHIE: Eh?

JOHNNY: You know, like Nostradamus. 'E was like this sixteenth-century astrologer. An' 'e wrote in one of 'is quatrains . . . that this goon called Hister would invade Poland. So Hitler reads that, and thinks, 'Hister: Hitler. Must mean me', and invades Poland. So when the guy prophesied that the world would end in 1999, which 'e did, does that therefore mean that we're fulfillin' the prophecy by precipitatin' the Apocalypse? Are you with me?

ARCHIE: Uh?

JOHNNY: Do you think the world will end in 1999?

(ARCHIE *tuts disdainfully and returns his attention to the street.*)

Listen, mate, what d'you think to this? Why don't you 'ave a little wander round and go look for the wee lassie, an' I'll

30

wait 'ere? And if she turns up, I'll keep 'er 'ere till you get
    back.

ARCHIE: What?

JOHNNY: 'Ow does that grab you?

ARCHIE: Are you gonna be here, aye?

JOHNNY: Yeah.

ARCHIE: Right. If she gets back, right, tell her to fuckin' wait here
    till I get back. If she wanders off, knock her oot. And slap her
    gob for me, right?

JOHNNY: Yeah, I'll tie her up.

ARCHIE: Aye. Are you gonna be here, aye?

JOHNNY: Yeah. Oh, listen. What's 'er name again?

ARCHIE: Maggie.

JOHNNY: (*Laughing*) Oh, yeah.

ARCHIE: Be back in a minute, right?

    (ARCHIE *hares off down the street, twitching as he goes.* JOHNNY
    leans against the wall and sighs.)

A while later. JOHNNY *is still in the same place. He approaches a
woman leaning at the other end of the same shop front. She is wearing
blue jeans and she has black hair.*

JOHNNY: Excuse me, love. Hallo?! Are you Maggie?

WOMAN: Piss off! (*She walks away.*)

Later still, JOHNNY *is still standing outside the shop. He is smoking a
cigarette. A girl with black hair arrives, scanning the now emptier street.*

JOHNNY: Oh, you're Maggie!

MAGGIE: Wha'?

JOHNNY: Is your name Maggie?

MAGGIE: How d'ye ken that?

JOHNNY: It's just a hunch. Are you looking for the, er . . . petulant
    dwarf?

MAGGIE: Eh?

JOHNNY: *Sprechen sie Deutsch?*

    (*She turns away.*)

MAGGIE: (*Shouting*) Archie!!

JOHNNY: Yeah, that's the fella. I was told to wait 'ere for you.
    You're Maggie, 'e's Archie, I'm nobody – e's gone off lookin'
    for you, love.

MAGGIE: What, you've seen 'um?

JOHNNY: Look, would you come and sit over 'ere, now?

MAGGIE: Fuck off, you dirty cunt!

(*She walks away.*)

JOHNNY: (*Laughing*) Yeah, well, I know I've not 'ad a bath for a
good few seasons, but there's no need to 'urt my feelin's.
'E'll be back in a minute!

(MAGGIE *turns round.*)

MAGGIE: What, he's been here?

(*She comes back.*)

JOHNNY: He's been 'ere. He's been there. He's been all over the
fuckin' shop.

MAGGIE: And did 'e 'ave the chips wi' 'um?

JOHNNY: He had a huge one on 'is shoulder.

MAGGIE: Fuckin' wee radge!

JOHNNY: Oh, come on. There's no need to knock the young lad.
He's a wonderful exponent of the old Socratic debate.

More time has passed and the street is even quieter. JOHNNY *and*
MAGGIE *are sitting side by side on the shop step.* JOHNNY *laughs a
little.*

JOHNNY: Listen, love. I've got this great idea. Why don't you
'ave a little wander round, see if you can find the wee lad, an'
I'll wait 'ere. An' if 'e turns up, I'll keep 'im 'ere till you get
back.

MAGGIE: I'm fuckin' starvin'.

JOHNNY: D'you wanna get somethin' to eat?

MAGGIE: He's got all the money, hasn't 'e?

JOHNNY: Who? Laughing Boy?

MAGGIE: Aye.

JOHNNY: Well, I've got a few bob on me.

MAGGIE: Aye, and what if 'e comes back and we're no here?

JOHNNY: We'll leave 'em a note.

MAGGIE: He'll no be able to read it.

JOHNNY: Well, we'll get 'im on his bleeper – come on . . .

(*They get up and go. A man sweeps the street.*)

*A short time later. A desolate, decaying urban place. Old arches.
Lights in the distance, perhaps by the river. Junk everywhere. Men*

hover round a fire, whilst a trio of others stride purposefully by. Some
desolate kids, probably homeless, squat by a wall with a dog.

JOHNNY *and* MAGGIE *are walking along.*

JOHNNY: Can you feel all those vibrations?

MAGGIE: Wha'?

JOHNNY: Just stand still a minute, love.

    (*They stop.*)

    Try and feel it through your feet. D'you not get all those
    tremblin's and rumblin's comin' up through your bones?

MAGGIE: Not really, no.

    (*They set off again.*)

JOHNNY: D'you not get like a sense of, like, a whole other world
    underneath all this? You know, like the guts of London?
    What with all the tube trains and everything, the city's
    viscera and the subterranean fuckin' fistulas and conduits
    and colons and bunkers and dungeons and tombs an' all
    that?

MAGGIE: What about hell? And the sewers, like?

JOHNNY: You know that wherever you are in London, right,
    you're only thirty feet away from a rat?

MAGGIE: Aye?

JOHNNY: Does that freak you out?

MAGGIE: Nah.

And now at the dead of night JOHNNY *and* MAGGIE *are crossing an*
old, narrow railway bridge.

JOHNNY: D'you believe in hell?

MAGGIE: Aye.

JOHNNY: So d'you believe in the devil?

MAGGIE: Aye.

JOHNNY: What d'you think 'e looks like?

MAGGIE: Looks like that, doesn' 'e? (*She shows him a small*
troll-like doll attached to her zip.)

JOHNNY: What, a little nudist homunculus with a pink quiff?

MAGGIE: No, 'e looks like a snake.

JOHNNY: Let's 'ave a look at that.

    (*They stop.* JOHNNY *holds the figure.*)

    It's Archie, isn't it? (*He makes it twitch.*)

MAGGIE: It's my good-luck charm. (*She takes it.*)

JOHNNY: 'As it brought you much?

MAGGIE: Has it fuck.

JOHNNY: Are you superstitious?

MAGGIE: No.

JOHNNY: What d'you wear a good-luck charm for, then?

MAGGIE: (*Moving off*) Are we gonna get something to eat or what?
(JOHNNY *follows. They descend some steps. Heavy graffiti
everywhere. They pass an ancient bag-lady, staggering up the
steps with her burden.*)
Have you ever seen a dead body?

JOHNNY: Only me own.

*Now they are at an all-night tea stall. The owner, fag in mouth, pours
milk from a bottle into a jug. An aggressive-looking youth hovers
behind JOHNNY. A plump young man with a scar and an oversized
cap stands next to MAGGIE, apparently ignoring her.*

JOHNNY: Where was you thinkin' of sleepin' tonight?

MAGGIE: Dunno.

JOHNNY: Where did you kip down last night?

MAGGIE: In the park.

JOHNNY: Was that not cold?

MAGGIE: Aye. Where are you thinkin' of sleepin', like?

JOHNNY: Wherever I drop. 'Ow old are you, love?

MAGGIE: Twenty-three.

JOHNNY: Do your mam and dad know you're down 'ere?

MAGGIE: No.

JOHNNY: Will they not be worried about you?

MAGGIE: No. How old are you, like?

JOHNNY: 'Ow old d'you think I am?

MAGGIE: About forty.

JOHNNY: I'm twenty-seven.

MAGGIE: Oh, get to fuck!

A little later. JOHNNY *and* MAGGIE *wander across a barren piece of
wasteground. Behind them rises the hollow shell of a vast, long-
forgotten building. A lone figure squats by a wall.*
MAGGIE *is holding a canned drink.*
Suddenly, ARCHIE *appears.*
The following exchange is shouted violently.

34

ARCHIE: Where the fuck 'a you been?

MAGGIE: Where the fuck 'a you been?

ARCHIE: Uh?

MAGGIE: I've been waitin' on yer!

ARCHIE: Fuckin' come here – (*He goes to hit her.*)

MAGGIE: Fuck off!

ARCHIE: Cunt! What the fuck you been doin', eh?

MAGGIE: You've got all the money.

> (*As he advances towards her and she retreats, they circle round* JOHNNY.)

ARCHIE: I've been fuckin' lookin' all over for yer.

MAGGIE: Aye, well, I was wi' him.

ARCHIE: Were you fuck!

MAGGIE: I fuckin' was!

ARCHIE: I was fuckin' wi' him!

MAGGIE: I was fuckin' wi' him!

ARCHIE: Daft cunt! (*He kicks her.*)

MAGGIE: Fuckin' ask him!

> (*She pushes* JOHNNY.)

ARCHIE: Fuck off!

MAGGIE: Fuckin' ask him!

ARCHIE: Fuckin' daft bitch!

MAGGIE: Where's my chips?

ARCHIE: Eh? That was fuckin' years ago.

> (*He kicks her again. She runs off.*)

MAGGIE: Aye, well, I was starvin' wasn't I?

> (*He chases after her.*)

ARCHIE: I'll fuckin' gi' yer fuckin' chips!

MAGGIE: Fuck off! Fuckin' leave us alone!

ARCHIE: Kick your fuckin' cunt . . .

> (*They disappear into the darkness.* JOHNNY *stands alone in the mist.*)

Next day. JOHNNY *leans in a doorway. Crowds of people of all kinds pass him by as they go about their business.*

Late afternoon, the same day. At the flat, in the kitchen. LOUISE *and* SOPHIE *are sitting at the table.* LOUISE *is leafing through Johnny's book.*

SOPHIE: Did he 'urt yer?

    (LOUISE *looks at* SOPHIE.)

LOUISE: What d'you mean?

SOPHIE: You know . . . when you were fuckin'.

LOUISE: Why, did he 'urt you?

SOPHIE: D'you think you were made for each other?

    (LOUISE *returns to the book.*)

LOUISE: Well, we went out for a year.

SOPHIE: A year?! Fuckin' 'ell – gimme a year! D'you ever feel like
    topping yourself?

    (LOUISE *puts down the book.*)

LOUISE: Oh, God! I wish I was at 'ome.

SOPHIE: Glad I'm not.

LOUISE: Yeah, well, I don't mean with me mum and dad. I just
    mean in Manchester.

SOPHIE: Oh, you reckon it's different there, do you?

LOUISE: Yeah – people talk to you.

SOPHIE: Well, I'm talkin' to you.

LOUISE: Yeah, but you talk a pile of shit.

SOPHIE: Don't matter where you are, anyway. You might as well
    be in Zimbabwe with Sandra.

(LOUISE *looks round the room.*)

LOUISE: Are you gonna do any washin' up before she gets back?

SOPHIE: Yeah, course I am. When is she gettin' back?

LOUISE: Sunday.

SOPHIE: Well, that's four fuckin' days away, innit?

That night. Late. JOHNNY *sits, huddled in the doorway of a modern office block. A taxi passes.* JOHNNY *is reading his pocket Bible.*)

JOHNNY: (*Aloud*) 'Thou shalt not consent unto Him, nor harken unto Him. Neither shall thine eye pity Him, neither shalt thou spare, neither shalt thou conceal 'Im. But thou shalt surely kill 'Im. Thy ha-'

(*A* SECURITY GUARD *now stands watching him from just behind the glass double doors. He taps on the glass.* JOHNNY *stops reading and taps back.* JOHNNY *coughs. The* GUARD *moves away a few feet.*)

JOHNNY: Lost me place now.

(*The* GUARD *takes out his key.*)

'And thou shalt stone 'Im with stones, that He die because He hath sought to thrust thee away from the Lord thy God. And –' Oh, fuckin' 'ell! Why 'ast thou forsaken me? Bastard!

(*The* GUARD *has unlocked the door and now comes out. He stops and looks at* JOHNNY. JOHNNY *returns his look.*)

GUARD: Mmm.

(*He strolls on to the pavement and glances up and down the street. Then he returns to* JOHNNY. *He stands, looking down at him.*)

JOHNNY: Is that it now, then? Are you through with the regulation pacin'? You're all set to deploy the fatuous sarcasm? Well . . . I've beaten you to it.

GUARD: Would you like a mint? (*He offers him one.*)

JOHNNY: Oh, what's this, new policy? Ply the culprit with menthol?

GUARD: Extra strong.

(JOHNNY *takes a mint.*)

I get through four packets of these a night.

JOHNNY: You wanna be careful, don't yer? I don't want your poxy mint. (*He throws it away.*)

GUARD: Oh? Waste not, want not.

JOHNNY: And other clichés.

37

GUARD: Ah – but a cliché is full of truth, otherwise it wouldn't be a cliché.

JOHNNY: Which is in itself a cliché.

GUARD: Tell me, have you read the Book of Hosea?

JOHNNY: What now?

GUARD: 'For they are the children of whores.'

JOHNNY: There's no need to get personal, mate. Look, will you stop fuckin' about? If you're gonna stick the boot in, will you get on with it?

(*The* GUARD *whose name* JOHNNY *will later discover to be Brian, again goes to the pavement and again has a look up and down the street. Then he returns to* JOHNNY. *Pause.*)

BRIAN: Have you got nowhere to go, then?

JOHNNY: Yeah . . . I've got an infinite number of fuckin' places to go. The problem is, where you stay. Are you with me?

BRIAN: Indeed. Yes.

JOHNNY: So listen, is there much security in this job?

BRIAN: Too much.

(JOHNNY *stands up and joins* BRIAN. *They look through the glass doors.*)

JOHNNY: And what is it that goes on in this particular post-modernist gas chamber?

BRIAN: Nothing. It's empty.

JOHNNY: So what is it that you're guardin'?

BRIAN: Space.

(JOHNNY *chortles.*)

JOHNNY: You're guardin' space? Well, that's stupid, innit, because someone could break in there, right, and steal all the fuckin' space, and you wouldn't know it 'ad gone, would you?

BRIAN: Good point. Night-night.

(*He goes in, and locks the door. Then he sits behind the reception desk, puts on his spectacles and proceeds to read his book. Almost immediately, he closes the book and replaces it with another.* JOHNNY *watches him as he reads. He stops for a moment and looks at* JOHNNY. *He takes off his spectacles. He pauses. Suddenly, he snaps the book shut, gets up, comes to the door, unlocks it and opens it.*
JOHNNY *picks up his bag.*)

JOHNNY: Yeah, all right, pal. I appreciate you've got a job to do,
an' it's MOVE ON! MOVE ON! MOVE ON! But it's
fuckin' freezin' out there, an' I was a Caesarian.

(*After another glance up and down the street,* BRIAN *comes back
into the lobby.*)

BRIAN: Come on, quick!

JOHNNY: What?

BRIAN: Come in.

(*Pause. Then* JOHNNY *advances cautiously.*)

JOHNNY: Are you serious? (*He crosses the lobby.*)

BRIAN: Through that door . . . smartish.

JOHNNY: There's a funny smell in 'ere.

BRIAN: Come on.

(BRIAN *leads* JOHNNY *through the door.*)

*Moments later. A large, empty, carpeted office space, brightly lit by
fluorescent strips.* BRIAN *is closing the venetian blinds on the street-
facing windows.*

JOHNNY: A bit of a waste of space, all this, in't it? (*He is standing
in the middle of the floor.*) You could sleep a thousand flea-
bitten tramps in 'ere. (*He looks at a display of exotic indoor
plants.*) And what's all that? You know they say it's a fuckin'
jungle out there? 'Ave you seen it in 'ere? I mean, where's
the bloody monkeys?

(*The blinds closed,* BRIAN *advances briskly towards* JOHNNY,
rubbing his hands enthusiastically. JOHNNY *retreats a pace,
dropping his bag to the floor.*)

Look, Dad, will you just back off?! What is it you're after?

BRIAN: You must be invisible.

JOHNNY: What?

BRIAN: I . . . must be seen. Follow me.

(*He scuttles out.* JOHNNY *hovers for a moment, gasping in
amused disbelief. Then he sets off, almost forgetting his bag. Just
as he arrives at the door,* BRIAN *reappears abruptly.* JOHNNY
drops his bag by the wall.)

Sit there.

(*He disappears again. Pause.* JOHNNY *remains standing.*)

JOHNNY: Am I allowed to smoke in here?

(BRIAN *is back behind the reception desk in the adjacent lobby.*)

BRIAN: No. You'll set off the alarm. Now, I'm not gonna look at you. It mustn't look like I'm talking to anybody. If you're seen in here . . . I'm out of a job. (*He puts on his spectacles.*) See what I mean?

JOHNNY: Well, if they see you talkin' to yourself like that, you'll be out of a job anyway. They'll come after you with a big butterfly net.

BRIAN: Oh, yes . . . (*He huddles over the desk and hides his face with his hand.*) I'll stand like this, then.
(JOHNNY *smiles.*)
Well, that's better, isn't it?

JOHNNY: What?

BRIAN: In out of the cold.

JOHNNY: Yeah. Yeah – thanks very much. (*He leans in the doorway.*) It's funny bein' inside in't it? 'Cos when you are inside, you're still actually outside, aren't you? And then you can say when you're outside, you're inside, because you're always inside your head. D'you follow that?

BRIAN: Yes. Sometimes when I'm sitting here, I turn the lights off – sit in the dark. That always makes me feel like I'm sitting outside. (*He still doesn't look at* JOHNNY, *nor does he for the rest of this scene.*)

JOHNNY: So what d'you do with yourself here of a night-time?

BRIAN: I read. And I think.

JOHNNY: What d'you think about?

BRIAN: I think about my life.

JOHNNY: And is that horrendous for you?

BRIAN: No! Certainly not!

JOHNNY: Is it horrendous for your wife? Are you married, mate?

BRIAN: Well . . . technically I'm married. Although my wife is 5,919 miles away, and I haven't seen her for thirteen years.

JOHNNY: It's all going very well, then? Where is she?

BRIAN: She's in Bangkok.

JOHNNY: Saucy! (*Reflective pause.*) They're not worth it, are they?

BRIAN: Whores and harlots.

JOHNNY: When was the last time you 'ad a fuck?
(BRIAN *doesn't reply.*)
Is that an embarrassin' question for you?

BRIAN: It is, rather – yes.
JOHNNY: I'm sorry.

A little later. More fluorescent lights flick on in the big office space.
BRIAN *enters eagerly, followed by* JOHNNY.
BRIAN: Step this way . . . I want to reveal to you the mysteries of
my trade. (*He stops by a pillar. He is holding a plastic black-
and-white electronic security device, about the size of a torch.*)
What d'you think that is?
JOHNNY: A, er, Dadaist nun?
BRIAN: Wrong. This little lady is the representative of my
employer.
JOHNNY: How d'you do, love?
BRIAN: Watch . . . (*He runs the thing across a small plastic plate on
the wall. It bleeps.*)
JOHNNY: Very Zen.
BRIAN: My existence at this moment on this spot is now trapped
and recorded. Twenty-three moments, twenty-three sites,
every two hours. That's my job.
JOHNNY: Well, could they not train a tall chimpanzee to do that?
Or a small chimpanzee with a bigger gizmo?
BRIAN: I expect they could . . . yes.
JOHNNY: What's your name, son?
BRIAN: Brian.
JOHNNY: Hallo, Brian – Johnny. Well, Brian, congratulations!
You've succeeded in convincin' me that you do 'ave the most
tedious fuckin' job in England.
(*Pause.*)
BRIAN: Come on.
(*They set off. A brief top-shot – i.e. we look down at them. As
they pass the exotic plants,* JOHNNY *momentarily mock 'hacks'
his way through the jungle.*)

Seconds later. They come through a door and proceed up some stairs.
BRIAN *stops suddenly and turns on* JOHNNY.
BRIAN: Yes! It is a boring job! Bloody boring, actually.
JOHNNY: All right! All right!
BRIAN: But all you can see is the tip of the iceberg. The present.
The tedious here and now. What you're incapable of seeing

is the rest of time – the rest of the iceberg. The past and the future. My future. Which is a very interesting place to be. And the good thing about this job is that it gives me time and space to contemplate the future at my leisure. Whilst the city sleeps. Free from the cacophonous curiosity of the hoi polloi. So you see . . . it's not a boring job. (*He sets off, but stops.*) And I'm not boring, either.

(*Now he disappears upstairs.* JOHNNY *gets out his cigarettes.*)

JOHNNY: Am I allowed to smoke on the stairs?

BRIAN: (*From above*) No. There's alarms all over the building.

(JOHNNY *puts away the cigarettes. Then he proceeds slowly up the stairs.*)

JOHNNY: So you think you can make the present palatable by projectin' into the future? You're livin' in the past, pal. It's the future that fucks you up, Brian. It's the . . . the maggot in the apple.

Moments later, they enter another empty, brightly lit space with white walls. They are both now walking quickly. BRIAN *strides ahead to repeat the electronic wall process.*

JOHNNY: See, you're all pissed off with the present, Bri, and there's nothing wrong with the present. The present's fine. The present's perfect. The present's peachy-fuckin'-creamy. The only thing wrong with the present is the bastard doesn't exist. Because the present is the future, and the future is the past. And it's all the same fuckin' bag of bones anyway. It's a constant process of comin' into bein' and passin' away, comin' into bein' and passin' away. The future is now.

BRIAN: But the present does exist. We're in it, now.

JOHNNY: You were just then when you said it, but you're not in it now, you're not in it now, you're not in it now. You're forever bein' kicked up the arse by the future. Are you with me?

BRIAN: That's what I mean. See, I'm in the present. But I'm not in the present. I'm in the future. Exactly.

(*He moves off. Still talking,* JOHNNY *follows him into an adjacent space where the lights are off. Soon* JOHNNY *comes to a halt. He is thus silhouetted against some windows that separate the lit space they have just left. Brian rejoins him.*)

JOHNNY: Has nobody not told you, Brian, that you've got this kind of gleeful preoccupation with the future? I wouldn't even mind but you don't even 'ave a fuckin' future. I don't 'ave a future. Nobody 'as a future. The party's over. Take a look around you, man. It's all breakin' up. Are you not familiar with the Book of Revelation of St John, the final book of the Bible, prophesying the Apocalypse?

(BRIAN *has come back to rejoin* JOHNNY. *They are both now in silhouette.*)

BRIAN: Yes. As it happens, I'm familiar with all the books of the Bible.

JOHNNY: I'm very happy for you. 'He forced everyone to receive a mark on his right hand, or on his forehead, so that no one shall be able to buy or sell, unless he has the mark, which is the name of the beast. Or the number of his name; and the number of the beast is six-six-six.'

BRIAN: Six-six-six. I know about it.

JOHNNY: Great!

BRIAN: I know about Nostradamus. Nostradamus talked about three brothers. Now, did he mean the Kennedy brothers, or was he talking about three bits of the Soviet Union? You see, you just can't tell.

JOHNNY: Fuck Nostradamus! I'm not talkin' about Nostradamus
or Mother Shipton or Russell Grant or Mystic fuckin' Meg –
I'm talkin' about the Holy fuckin' Book! What can such a
specific prophecy mean? What is the mark? Well, the mark,
Brian, is the bar code – the ubiquitous bar code that you'll find
on every bog-roll, on every packet of johnnies, on every poxy
pork pie. And every fuckin' bar code is divided into two parts
by three markers. And those three markers are always
represented by the number six. Six. Six. Six! Now what does
it say? 'No one shall be able to buy, or sell, without that mark.'
And now, what they're plannin' to do in order to eradicate all
credit-card fraud, and in order to precipitate a totally cashless
society, what they're plannin' to do, what they've already
tested on the American troops, they're gonna subcutaneously
laser-tattoo that mark on to your right hand or on to your
forehead. They're gonna replace plastic with flesh. Fact! In
the same Book of Revelation, when the seven seals are broken
open on the Day of Judgement, and the seven angels blow the
trumpets, when the third angel blows 'er bugle, 'Wormwood
will fall from the sky. Wormwood will poison a third part of all
the waters, and a third part of all the land, and many, many,
many, many people will die.' Now, d'you know what the
Russian translation for 'wormwood' is?

BRIAN: No.

JOHNNY: Chernobyl. Fact! On the 18th of August 1999, the
planets of our solar system are gonna line up into the shape of
a cross.

BRIAN: I don't believe in astrology.

JOHNNY: I'm not talkin' about astrology. I'm talkin' about
astronomy. They're gonna line up in the fixed signs of
Aquarius, Leo, Taurus and Scorpio, which just happen to
correspond to the four beasts of the Apocalypse, as
mentioned in the Book of Daniel. Another fuckin' fact!
D'you want me to go on? The end of the world is nigh, Bri.
The game is up!

BRIAN: I don't believe that. Life can't just come to a stop.
(*He moves off to a wall and repeats the electronic process.*
JOHNNY *joins him.*)

JOHNNY: All right, I'm not sayin' that life will end, or the world

45

will end, or the universe will cease to exist. But Man will cease to exist. Just like the dinosaurs passed into extinction, the same thing'll happen to us. We're not fuckin' important. We're just a crap idea!

BRIAN: I'm not gonna cease to exist. I'm gonna be here in the future. (*He moves off.*)

JOHNNY: What is this fuckin' fixation with the future?! (*He follows* BRIAN, *shouting.*) Listen, pal, I've got chronic systolic palpitations and acute fuckin' neuralgia! What about these toilets – can I smoke in 'ere? (*He has followed* BRIAN *into a corridor.*)

BRIAN: (*Unseen, shouting*) No, you fuckin' can't!!
(BRIAN *arrives at a lift and presses the button.* JOHNNY *arrives.*) Let me ask you a question.

JOHNNY: What?

BRIAN: Have you ever had the sense that you've lived in a time different from this one?

JOHNNY: What, you mean like in a past life?

BRIAN: Could be, yeah.

JOHNNY: Yeah, well, in my past life I was dead.

BRIAN: Ah, well, you see – I wasn't. I know I was here in the past, before I was born. So I know I'm gonna be here in the future after I've died.

JOHNNY: I see. And in this alternative existence, did you still 'ave the same noxious body odour?
(*The lift doors open.*)

BRIAN: There's no need to be personal. It's what I believe.
(*They enter the lift.*)

JOHNNY: Shall I tell you what I believe?

BRIAN: You don't believe anything.

JOHNNY: Oh, I do, Brian.

BRIAN: Yeah? What do you believe?
(*The lift doors close.*)

Inside the lift.

JOHNNY: Do you think that the amoeba ever dreamed that it would evolve into the frog? Or course it didn't. And when that first frog shimmied out of the water and employed its vocal cords in order to attract a mate or to retard a predator, d'you think that that frog ever imagined that that incipient croak would evolve into all the languages of the world, into all the literature of the world? 'Course it fuckin' didn't. And just as that froggy could never possibly have conceived of – of Shakespeare, so we can never possibly imagine our destiny.

(*The doors open.* BRIAN *emerges.*)

BRIAN: I know what my destiny is.

(JOHNNY *follows him, as he now checks out a bathroom.*)

JOHNNY: Yeah, but what you're experiencin', as far as I can gather with all these manifestations of, er – regression and precognition and transmigratory astral fuckin' chatterin's, is just the equivalent of that first primeval grunt. Because evolution isn't over. Man isn't the be-all and fuckin' end-all.

(BRIAN *turns out a light and walks past* JOHNNY.)

Look.

(BRIAN *stops.*)

If you take the whole of time represented by one year, we're only in the first few moments of the 1st of January. There's a long way to go. Only now we're not gonna sprout extra limbs and wings and fins because evolution itself is evolvin'. And whereas you, through some process of extra-sensory recall, might imagine that you were some – I dunno, some seventeenth-century little Dutch girl livin' in a windmill in Old Amsterdam, one day you'll realize that you've had not just one or two past or future existences, but that you were, and are, everybody and everything that 'as ever been, or will ever be.

(BRIAN *has gone into a second bathroom. Suddenly he rejoins* JOHNNY *at the door.*)

BRIAN: Hang on a minute . . . You've just contradicted yourself.

JOHNNY: Oh, and 'ow d'you make that out?

BRIAN: Downstairs you were predicting the end of the world. Now you're talking about the future. How d'you explain that, eh?

JOHNNY: Easy. When it comes, the Apocalypse itself will be part of the process of that leap of evolution.

BRIAN: Yeah . . . well, whatever happens, mankind will not cease to exist.

(He turns out the bathroom light and walks past JOHNNY, *who follows.)*

JOHNNY: He must. By the very definition of Apocalypse, Mankind must cease to exist, at least in a material form.

(BRIAN stops in another doorway.)

BRIAN: What d'you mean, in a material form?

JOHNNY: Well, 'e'll evolve.

BRIAN: What into?

JOHNNY: Into something that transcends matter. Into a species of pure thought. Are you with me?

BRIAN: Yeah. Like a ghost.

JOHNNY: No, not like a fuckin' ghost, you big girl's blouse! Into somethin' that's, like, well beyond our comprehension. Into a universal consciousness, into God. Who is. By the same principle that time is.

BRIAN: You don't believe in God.

(He goes through the door. JOHNNY *follows.)*

JOHNNY: 'Course I believe in God.

A little later. Surrounded by silver pipes and ducts, JOHNNY *and* BRIAN *are sitting at the top of a functional-looking service staircase. Their mood is now calmer and quieter.*

JOHNNY: You see . . . The thing is, Brian . . . that God is a hateful God. Must be . . . because if God is good, then why is there evil in the world? Why is there pain and hate and greed and war? It doesn't make sense. But if God is a nasty bastard, then you can say, why is there good in the world? Why is there love and hope and joy? Well, let's face it, good exists in order to be fucked up by evil. The very existence of good enables evil to flourish. Therefore . . . God is bad. And it doesn't matter how many past or future existences you have, because they're all gonna be riddled with grief and anguish and sickness and death. You see, Brian, God doesn't love you. God despises you. So there's no hope. And mankind is just a component of the device by which the devil creates itself. You with me? You see, what I'm saying, basically, is you can't make an omelette without crackin' a few eggs, and humanity is just a cracked egg. And the omelette . . . stinks.

48

BRIAN: Yeah.

Later still. Another empty space. JOHNNY *is following* BRIAN *slowly and silently along a row of windows. The dark room is illuminated only by the lights in the street far below.*

They come to a halt at a round window with closed venetian blinds. They are silhouetted, side by side.

JOHNNY: Oh. And what's through the round window? (*pause.*)
'Oo's that?

BRIAN: Good question.
(*We now see a* WOMAN *from their point of view. She is in a small window nearby. A light is on in her room. She is wearing a loose garment and appears to be dancing.*)

JOHNNY: 'Ave you seen 'er before?

BRIAN: Oh, yeah. She's there every night.
(*The two men watch her. The striped shadow of the venetian blind falls across their faces.*)

JOHNNY: Good-lookin' young girl, in't she?

BRIAN: She's all right.

JOHNNY: Does she ever 'ave fellers up there?

BRIAN: No.

JOHNNY: 'Ave you ever seen 'er like, you know, totally naked?

BRIAN: Once. What's she up to, eh? I mean, what's her game, taunting people in the middle of the night, eh?

(JOHNNY *adjusts the blinds. She is playing with her hair.*)

JOHNNY: She probably gets a kick out of it. Like you get a kick out o' watchin' 'er.

BRIAN: I'm doing no such thing.

JOHNNY: Well, I am. 'Ave you got a 'ard-on?

BRIAN: No. I haven't, as a matter of fact.

JOHNNY: You wouldn't tell me if you'ad, would you?

BRIAN: No, I don't think I would.

Now JOHNNY *is once again standing with* BRIAN *on the front doorstep of the building. It is still night.* BRIAN *is holding a plastic lunch-box and they are each munching a sandwich.*

JOHNNY: Did you make these yourself?

BRIAN: I did, yeah.

JOHNNY: I thought so. (*He glances around the street.*) Well, listen, I might be back in a couple of minutes.

(BRIAN *laughs briefly.*)

BRIAN: Be good. If you can't be good, be careful!

JOHNNY: And other clichés.

BRIAN: Yeah.

JOHNNY: Well . . . Tatty-bye, Bri.

(*He walks off.* BRIAN *watches him go.*)

BRIAN: Yes. (*He glances the other way up the street.*)

Somewhere else in the city. A black Porsche races round a couple of corners. Inside, JEREMY *is driving and talking aggressively into his mobile phone. An attractive, very young, smartly dressed and quite innocent-looking* WOMAN *sits beside him, looking discreetly out of her side window.*

JEREMY: Charles? What?!! *Mais il est où alors? Écoute, je ne sais pas qui vous êtes.* 'Allo? Look what the fuck's going on? Where the bloody hell's Dorfman? The bastard's cost me thirty grand already!!

(*The* WOMAN *looks at him.*)

Quoi?! Qu'est-ce qui se passe? FUCK!! (*He thumps the steering wheel violently.*) Sorry about that . . .

(*The* WOMAN *smiles bravely, but the smile dissolves into a look of suppressed panic, as the journey continues.*)

50

Meanwhile, JOHNNY *has gone to visit the* WOMAN *in the window. She opens her front door. Though attractive, she is actually older than she looked from a distance. She is holding a cigarette.*

JOHNNY: Oh, I'm sorry, love, er . . . That's not you on the top floor, is it? Dancin'?

WOMAN: Yeah, why?

JOHNNY: Oh, right, erm . . . You're a lovely mover. I'm sorry, pet. I'm er . . . freakin' you out.

(*The* WOMAN *has stopped looking at him.*)

WOMAN: Where's Bhapu?

JOHNNY: Bhapu?

WOMAN: It's cold.

JOHNNY: Listen, I'd better explain myself – you see me brother's workin' as an insecurity guard in that fuckin' monstrosity round the back, and we can see straight into your room. It's very nice. Anyway, 'e's got 'is boss comin' round. So 'e's told me to schlep round the streets for a couple of hours, and I said I'd come and say 'ello to Isadora Duncan. Keep you company. (*She is vaguely amused.*)
I know it's a bit cheeky but, er . . . I'm a cheeky young monkey!

WOMAN: D'you wanna come in?

JOHNNY: Is that all right?

Now the WOMAN *is leading* JOHNNY *up a dimly lit, dank, decaying staircase. She stops on the landing and strokes his moustache.*

WOMAN: How long you been growing that?

JOHNNY: About two inches.

WOMAN: It's nice.

(*She carries on.* JOHNNY *follows.*)

JOHNNY: You've 'ad a few, an't you, love?

(*She stops at another door.*)

WOMAN: D'you wanna come in?

JOHNNY: Thought you'd never ask.

(*They proceed down a short corridor towards her room.*)

A minute or two later. JOHNNY *sits at a cluttered table, on which there are, amongst other things, a table-lamp, which is on, and a bottle each of vodka and tonic water.*

JOHNNY: Am I allowed to smoke in 'ere?

WOMAN: Yeah.

JOHNNY: Thank Christ for that.

WOMAN: D'you wanna drink?

(She picks up the bottle of vodka and pours a drop into each of two tumblers. JOHNNY lights a cigarette. The WOMAN laughs slightly.)

JOHNNY: I think I better 'ad, don't you? Got a bit of fuckin' catchin' up to do, an't I? *(He raises his glass.)* Here's to the monarchy!

(The WOMAN laughs slightly again. Then she walks to the window and looks out. In the distance BRIAN can be seen dimly in the round window, but she doesn't notice him.)

What's funny?

WOMAN: I'm not laughin'.

JOHNNY: So d'you live 'ere on yer own, yeah? *(He picks up a paperback book.)* Is this what you're readin'?

(She turns round.)

Jane Austen by Emma.

WOMAN: It's my favourite book.

(JOHNNY puts it down.)

JOHNNY: Is it really? I don't read much, meself. *(He flicks through several other books.)*

A little later. The WOMAN is leaning over a hand-basin, as if to be sick. Then she looks in a mirror above the sink and wipes her face.

JOHNNY: You from Ireland?

WOMAN: No. Why?

JOHNNY: What's that, a damp patch?

(The WOMAN looks round. JOHNNY is referring to an old map of Ireland on the wall next to where she is standing. She moves nearer to it.)

WOMAN: Oh . . . I never noticed that before. *(She studies it closely.)*

A little more time has passed. Now the WOMAN is sitting on the edge of her bed. She drops shakily on to the floor and staggers across the room on all fours to JOHNNY, who is still in the armchair.

JOHNNY: 'Ow's it goin' inside there?

(*He strokes her head. She bites his finger gently and kisses his hand.* JOHNNY *glances at the bed in a detached way.*)

WOMAN: Baby . . . Baby. (*She staggers back and sits on the bed. She takes off her dressing gown.*)

JOHNNY: 'Ow old are you, love? It's funny, 'cos from over there you look a lot younger. I think me big brother's quite taken with you.

(*She takes a sip of vodka.*)

'E's up there every night, 'avin' a bit of a wank about yer. Are you with me?

(*She drinks, but says nothing.* JOHNNY *gets up. Slowly, he walks towards her. She puts down her drink. He stands over her. Gently but firmly, he kicks her legs slightly wider apart. He caresses her hair. He kneels down before her. He cups her face in his hands. He kisses her on the mouth, gently at first, but his grip on her hair becomes gradually tighter. He starts to jolt her head a little. He is hurting her. She grabs his wrists to try to pull his hands off. She gasps with pain. Suddenly, he stops the kiss, but he keeps hold of her hair.*)

What's the matter?

WOMAN: Don't do that.

JOHNNY: What, that? (*He jolts her head.*) Or that? (*He jolts it again.*) Don't you like that? (*He jolts it back.*)

WOMAN: You don't 'ave to 'urt me.

(*He brings his face close to hers.*)

JOHNNY: I'm sorry.

(*He jolts her head, then lets go of her hair. Pause. She looks at him for a few moments in a distraught way. Then she slowly unbuttons her top.* JOHNNY *watches her. He folds his arms and gazes up in Brian's general direction. Suddenly and abruptly, he pulls down her sleeves and her bra-straps, revealing her breasts. She gasps. Pause. He runs his finger down her chest and caresses her nipple. Then he runs his finger back up to her neck and takes hold of it. He leans forward to kiss her on the lips again. He pushes her onto the bed, so that she is lying on her back. He leans over her. She looks away. He buries his face in her shoulder and begins to massage her breast. He kisses her neck gently.*)

WOMAN: Bite me.

(*He stops. He sits up slightly and looks at her.*)

Fuckin' bite me! Come on! (*She punches him hard.*)

JOHNNY: Ey!

(*He gets on top of her and pins down her arms. She is still trying to thump him.*)

Ey! Ey!

(*She stops. Then she tries to break free. He lies on her, perhaps intent on biting her. She tries to fight him off. She gasps and moans. They struggle on the bed, which we now see for a moment through the window, as from Brian's point of view.*
Suddenly, JOHNNY *releases her and she turns over on her side, revealing a small skull-and-crossbones tattoo on her back, near her shoulder.* JOHNNY *laughs drily.*)

'Oo's this? 'Oo's THIS?!!

(*He head-butts the skull, and pulls her on to her back again, forcefully. He hovers over her for a second. Then he sits up abruptly. She gasps. He looks at her. He gets up. He goes to the other window (the room has two). He looks up at* BRIAN, *whom we see, still watching from the round window.*
Now we see JOHNNY, *framed in his window, again from Brian's point of view. He is looking towards* BRIAN. *He glances in the direction of the* WOMAN, *then back at* BRIAN. *Then he sits in the armchair and watches the* WOMAN.*)

A short time later. The WOMAN *is now sitting on the edge of her bed again. She loosens her necklace of beads and mouths an erotic exhortation to* JOHNNY. *He gazes at her with a mixture of amusement and disgust. Without taking her eyes off him, she puts up her hair and continues to mouth loving words. For a moment, she can't find her hair-grip. But she finds it and fixes it.* JOHNNY *begins to look slightly horrified. She strokes her front curls as part of her 'seduction' and continues to mouth words. She adopts a 'sexy' pose, one hand held on her head.*

JOHNNY: I can't, love. You look like me mother.

> *(She freezes, her hand still on her head. Slowly, she begins to sob.)*

Some time later. The lights in the room are now out. The WOMAN *is lying on her bed with her bare back to* JOHNNY. *He is still in the chair. He isn't looking at her. He is drowsy.*

JOHNNY: D'you think you can recapture your youth by fuckin' it? You don't want to fuck me – you'll catch something cruel.

Early next morning. JOHNNY *is asleep in the chair. He wakes up and blinks in the cold, grey light. He looks at the* WOMAN. *She is fast asleep under her duvet. He picks up his bag. Keeping an eye on the* WOMAN, *he quietly unzips it. He picks up four of her paperback books and places them in his bag.*

Shortly after this, JOHNNY *is standing on the corner of a stark, narrow street.* BRIAN *is walking towards him. He arrives. He stops. He is wearing his overcoat and a beret, and is carrying a shoulder-bag and a newspaper.*

JOHNNY: *Bonjour.*

BRIAN: What's goin' on? What're you doin' 'ere?

JOHNNY: Well . . . you see . . . I was over 'ere, like this *(Takes one pace to his right)*, but that didn't work for me, so I thought I'd try it over 'ere *(Back to his first position)*, but I don't think there's much future in this one either. Fuckin' 'ell! 'Ave you got any suggestions?

BRIAN: No.

JOHNNY: So what do you do now?

BRIAN: I'm gonna get some breakfast.

JOHNNY: Yeah, I could do with somethin' to eat. Can I come with
    yer?
BRIAN: Well, have you got any money?
JOHNNY: No.
BRIAN: Well, how are you gonna pay for it?
JOHNNY: I'm not.
BRIAN: Well . . . I'm hungry.
    (*He walks off.* JOHNNY *follows.*)

*A few minutes later. In a café of the 'greasy spoon' variety. White
tiles. Formica-top tables.* JOHNNY *and* BRIAN *are sitting at a table in
the corner.* BRIAN *is flicking through his newspaper.* JOHNNY *is
smoking.*
BRIAN: Did you have to go and beat her up?
JOHNNY: I never beat 'er up.
BRIAN: You shagged her, though?
JOHNNY: No.
    (BRIAN *takes off his reading glasses and looks at* JOHNNY.
    JOHNNY *stares back at him.* BRIAN *looks away.*)
    You don't believe me, do you?
    (BRIAN *isn't sure. He puts on his spectacles.*)
    She's older than you.
BRIAN: (*Under his breath*) Bollocks.
    (*A girl has arrived with Brian's breakfast. She is wearing a long
    skirt.*)
GIRL: Poached egg. (*She puts down the plate, and a knife and fork,
    and walks away.*)
JOHNNY: That skirt's a bit short, innit, love? 'T's disgraceful.
    (*The* GIRL *looks at* JOHNNY *as she goes behind the counter.
    Perhaps the faintest glimmer of a smile, but maybe not.*
    BRIAN *takes a folded piece of paper out of a pocket. He holds it
    out to* JOHNNY. JOHNNY *takes it.*)
    What's this?
BRIAN: That's where I'm gonna live.
    (*It is a photograph of a small, isolated and very basic cottage next
    to the sea.*)
JOHNNY: Where is it?
BRIAN: Ireland. I've lived in that cottage before.
JOHNNY: What, in one of your past lives?

BRIAN: Yes, as a matter of fact.

(*He sprinkles salt on his egg.* JOHNNY *studies the photo.*)

JOHNNY: Fuckin' shit-hole, innit?

(*He puts it down.* BRIAN *picks it up and looks at it.*)

BRIAN: (*Muttering*) Don't waste your life.

JOHNNY: What?

BRIAN: (*measured*) Don't . . . waste . . . your life.

(JOHNNY *looks at* BRIAN, *perhaps a touch nonplussed.*)

Outside the plain little Jubilee Café, as it is called. BRIAN *leaves.*

Inside, JOHNNY *is standing at the counter. The* GIRL *is behind it, working.*

JOHNNY: What time does this place close?

GIRL: Four o'clock.

JOHNNY: Er, listen . . . Can you tell me where I can get somethin' to eat round 'ere?

GIRL: (*Giggling*) What?

JOHNNY: You've got a very nice smile.

GIRL: 'Ave I?

JOHNNY: Oh, yeah.

(*He leaves. She watches him go.*)

Later. Two men in white coats push trolleys briskly across a spacious landscape of confident modern office blocks. JOHNNY, *his bag on his shoulder, heads towards a distant cluster of gleaming white skyscrapers.*

Now, sitting in front of a vast concrete-and-glass building, JOHNNY *reads a paperback. He is smoking.*

And now he is strolling past a smart, Georgian town-house. A quite new Rolls-Royce is parked on the corner. JOHNNY *stops to look at it. The bald, dozing* CHAUFFEUR *wakes up and looks at* JOHNNY. *He puts on his uniform cap.*

CHAUFFEUR: Sorry, sir.

(*He gets out of the car and opens the rear door.* JOHNNY *looks at him.*)

I'll take that, sir.

(*He takes Johnny's bag from his shoulder.* JOHNNY *gets into the car.*)

Your lady companion's joinin' you, sir?

JOHNNY: Er, no – she can't make it today, pal, the old, er, sciatica's playin' up an' everythin', you know?

(*He gets out a cigarette. The* CHAUFFEUR *drops his bag on the pavement.*)

CHAUFFEUR: Come on . . .

JOHNNY: What?

CHAUFFEUR: Out the car.

JOHNNY: But I've only just got in the car.

CHAUFFEUR: (*Shouting*) Get out of the fuckin' car!!!

(JOHNNY *sniggers.*)

JOHNNY: All right, Parker, keep your 'air on.

(*He gets out. The* CHAUFFEUR *slams the rear door, gets back into his seat and slams his door.* JOHNNY *retrieves his bag.*

Well . . . that was lovely. Thank you.

(*The* CHAUFFEUR *closes his window.*)

Keep in touch. (JOHNNY *walks off.*)

Meanwhile, back at Sophie, Louise and Sandra's flat, SOPHIE *is climbing the steps outside the house.*

Inside, she opens the fridge. In the door are a can of lager and a bottle of champagne. She takes the lager and inspects the champagne. She closes the door.

As she opens the can, she strolls towards the living room. She stops in the doorway.

SOPHIE: Ooh, fuck!

(*A man is sitting on the sofa with his back to her. He looks round. It is* JEREMY. *He gets up and starts towards her. He is wearing a smart suit and tie.*)

'Oo are you?

JEREMY: Sebastian Hawks. Nice to meet you. (*He holds out his hand, which she doesn't take.*)

SOPHIE: Yeah . . . Er, what're you doin' 'ere?

JEREMY: I'm an acquaintance of Sandra's.

SOPHIE: Oh, yeah?

JEREMY: I just popped round to say hallo.

SOPHIE: Well, Sandra's away at the moment, actually.

JEREMY: Really? I hope you don't mind, but I helped myself to a beer. (*He strolls back into the middle of the room.*)

SOPHIE: Yeah, I noticed. Is that your champagne an' all?
JEREMY: You like champagne, do you?
SOPHIE: Yeah . . . I do, as it 'appens.
JEREMY: This is a very nice flat, don't you think?
SOPHIE: 'Ow d'you get in 'ere?

A few minutes later. JEREMY *is sitting on the sofa with his lager.*
SOPHIE *is in an armchair with hers. She has taken off her cap and jacket.*
JEREMY: Tell me, d'you have any problems with the central
    heating?
SOPHIE: Oh, are you the plumber?
JEREMY: Let's just say I've got a vested interest in the property.
SOPHIE: Fuckin' 'ell, you're the landlord.
JEREMY: I'd rather you thought of me as a friend.
SOPHIE: Oh, shit! What, is Sandra behind on the rent or
    somethin'?
JEREMY: Was your tattoo painful?
SOPHIE: Yeah.
JEREMY: Good. You're very beautiful, aren't you?
SOPHIE: Am I?
JEREMY: In a quirky sort of way. (*He takes a sip of beer.*)

A few more minutes have passed. JEREMY *is still sitting, but* SOPHIE *is walking about.*
JEREMY: Are you a nurse?
    (*She stands in front of him.*)
SOPHIE: Yeah. Psychiatric.
    (JEREMY *sniggers.*)
JEREMY: These are a very fetching pair of tights.
    (*Fishnet, with some worn holes. He feels them.*)
SOPHIE: Oh, you like them, do yer, Mr Landlord? Can we 'ave that
    champagne now, please?
    (*He continues to stroke the tights.*)
JEREMY: Did you buy them like this or are the holes self-inflicted?
SOPHIE: No. A spider spun them, and that's where 'e 'ad a
    tea-break.
    (*Suddenly, and violently,* JEREMY *rips an enormous hole in the
    tights, giggling as he does so.*)

59

Fuckin' 'ell! That's a bit excessive, innit?

JEREMY: I rather like this belt too.

(*He pulls her towards him.*)

SOPHIE: Oh, God! 'Ere we go. (*She looks towards the window and sighs.*)

Late afternoon. Back at the café. JOHNNY *is sitting at a table. The* GIRL *is by the door. She is wearing her coat.*

JOHNNY: Er, excuse me, where d'you think you're going'?

GIRL: I'm goin' home.

JOHNNY: What, are you leavin' me?

GIRL: Yeah.

JOHNNY: I've come all this way to see you and you're goin'! I can't believe it, I'm stunned, I'm flabbergasted.

GIRL: Shall I get you a tissue?

JOHNNY: Sounds promisin'. Do you live nearby?

GIRL: I might do.

JOHNNY: I mean, is it within walking distance?

(*She opens the door and leaves.* JOHNNY *gets up and follows her out.*)

No . . . 'Cos you see I've got this fascination with all things peripatetic.

GIRL: (*To someone inside*) See yer!

JOHNNY: I'm cheeky, aren't I?

(*She puts on a black woolly hat.*)

'Ave you stolen the teacosy? Love, people can see you wearin' that thing, are you not embarrassed? No?

(*He stops, but she walks down the street. He catches her up.*)

Meanwhile, at the flat. Sandra's bedroom. JEREMY, *wearing only his underpants, is lying on his back on Sandra's bed.* SOPHIE, *wearing only her bra and pants, is kneeling over him, whipping him strenuously with her long hair, working her way up from his legs to his chest.*

She stops, exhausted, and flops down beside him on the bed, face down.

JEREMY: Don't give up.

(*He grabs her roughly by the hair. She gasps and howls with pain. He pulls her head back on to his chest. She resumes the whipping.*)

60

(*A bit later.* JEREMY *snatches Sandra's nursing uniform from its hanger. He throws it at* SOPHIE, *who is lying crumpled on the bed. She is no longer wearing her bra.*)

JEREMY: Put this on.

SOPHIE: Oh, what? We're gonna play doctors and nurses now, are we?

JEREMY: Hurry up!

(*She puts on the uniform, pulling it over her head.*)

SOPHIE: Oh, this is ridiculous. Listen . . . I'm really sorry, right? But I've had a bit of a rough week . . . and I just don't think I can go through with this.

(*She attempts to go.* JEREMY *grabs hold of her. He throws her back on to the bed and jumps on top of her. He goes for her neck. She screams.*)

Oh . . . no! No!

(*Shortly after this,* JEREMY *has* SOPHIE *forced into a kneeling position on the bed. He is gripping her hair. She is wearing the uniform. He is naked. He is taking her from behind, aggressively, violently, horribly. He is grunting.* SOPHIE *is screaming desperately.*)

Fuck off! leave me alone! No! You fuckin' bastard!!

(*It is still daylight.*)

At the same moment, JOHNNY, *having gone back with the café* GIRL *to her place, is sitting at her kitchen table. She is standing by the cooker and the cupboards. There is a pause.*

GIRL: D'you want some beans?

JOHNNY: Yeah, cheers. So what would you be doin' now if I wasn't 'ere?

GIRL: Dunno. Havin' a shower, relaxin'.

JOHNNY: I could do with a shower myself. I haven't washed for about a week. As you've probably noticed.

GIRL: Well, you can 'ave one if you like.

JOHNNY: Are you sure?

GIRL: Yeah. Bathroom's just here.
(She moves quietly towards the bathroom. JOHNNY *follows.)*

JOHNNY: Fuckin' 'ell. What did I do to deserve you, love?

GIRL: *(From the bathroom)* Just press this button.
(In the bathroom. She is coming out as JOHNNY *arrives. She stops.)*

JOHNNY: Now, listen . . . You're not gonna creep up on me with a big knife dressed up as your mother, are you?
(She half smiles.)

GIRL: No.
(Pause. Then he stands aside for her. She leaves the bathroom.)

JOHNNY: Although it looks like you already are dressed up as your mother.
(She looks at him, then closes the bathroom door.)

Back in the kitchen, she unscrews a vodka bottle. JOHNNY *pops his head round the bathroom door. She hides the bottle quickly.*

JOHNNY: Can I have me bag? It's got me duck in it.
(She puts down the bottle and picks up the bag. She offers it to him. He takes it.)
Ta.
(They look at each other. She lowers her eyes. He goes back into the bathroom. She pauses for a moment. Then she goes back to the vodka and pours some into a glass. She puts down the bottle and has a sip.)

A few minutes later. Johnny is asleep in the bath.

Later still. It is still light. JOHNNY *has had his bath and is dressed. He wanders into the girl's living room. He is drying his hair with a towel. The* GIRL *hovers in the doorway.* JOHNNY *stops and registers the mantelpiece. This is a rather ornate, baroque–art-nouveau affair and boasts a neat, if busy, display of various Greek classical and other assorted ornaments.*

JOHNNY: Oh, dear. 'Oo lives 'ere, then? Zeus? Is all this stuff yours? (*He goes over to the mantelpiece.*)

GIRL: No.

JOHNNY: All these pseudo-Doric midgets with their novelty underpants. (*He inspects a young warrior surmounting a clock.*) Oh, and look at this one, touchin' time with a bargepole. I wouldn't. (*He looks round and leans on the mantelpiece.*) Is 'e a . . . home-owner-sexual, yeah?

GIRL: What do you think?

JOHNNY: Where is 'e?

GIRL: They're in America.

JOHNNY: They?

GIRL: Yeah.

JOHNNY: When are they gettin' back?

GIRL: Dunno.

JOHNNY: And they're just lettin' you stop 'ere for nothin', yeah?

GIRL: Yeah. I don't know them.

JOHNNY: I don't know . . . I find all this a bit sad.

GIRL: Why?

JOHNNY: No, I don't mean that to sound . . . homophobic. I mean, I like *The Iliad*. And *The Odyssey*. (*Laughs.*) D'you get that?

GIRL: No.

(JOHNNY *turns his attention to a well-stocked bookshelf.*)

JOHNNY: So . . . 'ave you, er, read many of these books?

GIRL: No, I haven't.

JOHNNY: Oh. I've read quite a few. Oh, look! (*He gets out a small paperback.*) D'you get it now?
(*It's Homer:* The Iliad.)
D'you know this?
(*She shakes her head.*)

JOHNNY: I bet you do. You've most likely done it at school – you just can't remember. You know, like, er, Achilles' heel, the Wooden Horse, Helen of Troy. You know them?

GIRL: Yeah.

JOHNNY: Yeah, well, that's all it is. Good stuff. Cyclops. Oh, hallo
... it's, er ... Pizza Deliveryman.

(*A muscular ancient Greek discus-thrower, part of a table-lamp.*
JOHNNY *laughs.*)

GIRL: D'you want those beans?

JOHNNY: Oh, yeah, I forgot.

(*The* GIRL *goes out of the room.*)

Now it is dark. LOUISE *climbs the steps outside the house. She gets out
her key, opens the front door and goes inside.*

As she comes up the lower stairs, JEREMY *is coming down from
upstairs. He is naked but for his underpants. He carries his jacket in one
hand. They meet on the landing.*

JEREMY: Sebastian Hawks. Good evening. Very nice to meet you,
Louise.

(*He shakes her hand.*)

LOUISE: Oh, very nice to meet you.

JEREMY: I've heard a lot about you.

(*He goes.* LOUISE *calls upstairs.*)

LOUISE: Sophie?

(*Sophie's voice, a little frail, comes from nearby.*)

SOPHIE: Yeah? Yeah, I'm in 'ere.

(LOUISE *goes to the living-room door.* JEREMY *has sat on the sofa.*
SOPHIE *is hunched over a cushion on the floor by the wall. She is
very shaky. She is still wearing the nurse's outfit.*)

LOUISE: Oh ... are you all right?

SOPHIE: (*Bitterly*) I've never been better.

JEREMY: (*Perkily*) We've had a very interesting afternoon, haven't
we, Sophie?

SOPHIE: It's been fascinatin'!

(JEREMY *sniggers.* LOUISE *leaves.* JEREMY *then counts out a
substantial amount of paper money from his wallet. He stands up
and sprinkles the money all over* SOPHIE.)

JEREMY: For services rendered.

(SOPHIE *gets up and pushes him out of the way.*)

SOPHIE: Fuck off!

(*She runs out of the room, in distress.* JEREMY *sniggers. She
staggers into the kitchen, where* LOUISE *is wiping up a mug.*

64

SOPHIE *sits down, coughs a little and does up her buttons.*)
LOUISE: 'Oo's your friend?
SOPHIE: 'E's the landlord, in' 'e?
LOUISE: 'Oose landlord?
SOPHIE: Our fuckin' landlord.
LOUISE: Oh, get out o' town!
SOPHIE: Ask 'im.
LOUISE: What're you wearin' Sandra's uniform for?
SOPHIE: I don't wanna talk about it, all right?
LOUISE: Well, d'you wanna cup o' tea?
SOPHIE: Yeah.
LOUISE: So 'ave you been sittin' on 'is face all afternoon?
SOPHIE: I don't need this.
LOUISE: Jesus Christ, I get 'ome from work, all I wanna do is put
        me feet up and watch the telly, not get involved in one of your
        orgies. D'you know what I mean? (*Suddenly she notices
        Sophie's bruises. Her mood changes abruptly.*) What 'appened to
        your arm? Sophie, what's been goin' on?
        (JEREMY *saunters in, in his underpants.*)
JEREMY: Have you put the kettle on?
LOUISE: Yeah.
JEREMY: Any chance of a coffee, Louise?
LOUISE: Yeah, sure.
        (JEREMY *sits on a stool.*)
JEREMY: These are a very nice pair of shorts. (*He feels the bottom of
        Louise's garment.*)
LOUISE: Would you take your 'ands off me, please?
        (*He does so.*)
JEREMY: I apologize.

A short time later. The living room. JEREMY *is now lounging full-
length, on the sofa. He is still wearing only his pants.* LOUISE *and*
SOPHIE *arrive briskly from upstairs. They are carrying Jeremy's
belongings.*
LOUISE: Right, pal. 'Ere's your clothes, get your kit on and sling
        yer 'ook. (*She throws his assorted things over the back of the sofa.*)
SOPHIE: 'Ere's your shoes, mate.
        (*She drops them on the floor. The two women go and stand
        together on the other side of the room.*)

JEREMY: Hope I haven't given you AIDS, Sophie.

LOUISE: (*Speaking together*) Jesus Christ.

SOPHIE: Fuckin' 'ell! Are you serious?

JEREMY: Merely jesting.

LOUISE: Very funny.

JEREMY: Mind you, I think AIDS is rather healthy, in its way.

LOUISE: You what?

JEREMY: I realize that's not the fashionable thing to say, of course.

LOUISE: No. It's not.

JEREMY: But the world is overcrowded, isn't it? It could do with a bit of pruning.

SOPHIE: Fuckin' better be jokin'.

JEREMY: You're not going to have children, are you, Louise?

LOUISE: I might do, one day.

JEREMY: I loathe children, I must say.

LOUISE: I bet they're not too keen on you, neether.

(JEREMY *laughs*.)

JEREMY: I'm sure you like fucking, don't you, Louise?

LOUISE: Are you goin'?

JEREMY: I'm rather enjoying myself, actually.

LOUISE: Yeah, well, we're not.

JEREMY: That's a pity.

LOUISE: Look, you may be the landlord from hell, but that doesn't give you the right to lie on our couch.

JEREMY: Whose couch?

LOUISE: D'you want me to phone the police?

JEREMY: Be my guest.

LOUISE: Right.

LOUISE *walks out of the room.* SOPHIE *follows her into the kitchen. They stop by the phone.*

SOPHIE: Listen, I can't 'ave them in 'ere?

LOUISE: Why not?

SOPHIE: They're gonna take one look at 'im in 'is suit and one look at us, an' 'oo d'you think they're gonna believe? There's fuckin' dope all over the place.

LOUISE: Well, we're just windin' 'im up – 'e's lovin' this. What are we gonna do?

66

(JEREMY *lies smugly on the sofa.*)

Meanwhile, JOHNNY *is lying on a cushion on the floor in front of the camp mantelpiece. An electric fire burns in the grate. The* GIRL *sits in an armchair, hugging a cushion. They each have a tumbler of vodka.*

JOHNNY: It's very peaceful in 'ere, isn't it? (*He sips his drink.*)

GIRL: I suppose so. (*Pause.*) Are you warm enough?

JOHNNY: Yeah, it's nice – thanks. It's funny, 'cos the silence usually freaks me out. You start to pick up on all the small sounds, you know what I mean? Like that clock.
(*The* GIRL *looks at it: a wall-clock, gold, with twelve pointed spikes, spoked like rays of the sun.*)

GIRL: I hate that fuckin' clock.

JOHNNY: Of course you do – it's a clock. Is it all right if I stay here the night?
(*Pause.*)

GIRL: 'Ve you ever 'ad a dog?

JOHNNY: No. I don't like dogs.

GIRL: Why?

JOHNNY: Well, they're either vicious or daft. (*He lights a cigarette.*) Why, 'ave you?

GIRL: Yeah.

JOHNNY: Is it dead now?

GIRL: Yeah.

JOHNNY: Did you bury it?

GIRL: I dunno, me dad took it.

JOHNNY: And what about you? Would you like to be buried or cremated?

GIRL: I couldn't give a shit.
(JOHNNY *chortles.*)

JOHNNY: I 'ad this, er, dream the other night, about these two skeletons havin' a fuck. It was a right bloody racket – woke me up.
(*The* GIRL *sips some vodka.*)

GIRL: 'Ave you got a photo of your mam?
(JOHNNY *laughs.*)

JOHNNY: What, on me?

GIRL: Yeah.

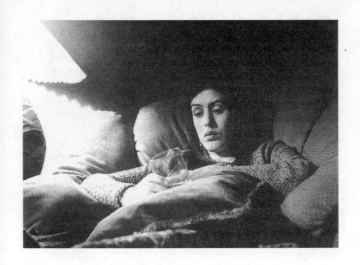

JOHNNY: No. But I think you might find one over at the
newsagent's, on the top shelf.

GIRL: D'you want some beans?

   (JOHNNY *looks at her. She looks away. He sits up.*)

JOHNNY: You've got a very sad face.

GIRL: 'Ave I? (*She covers her eyes. She is on the edge of tears.*)

JOHNNY: It's all right, I mean, I find that attractive. But that's
   me.

   (*She starts crying.*)

   So, 'ave you got a boyfriend or anythin'?

   (*She tries to pull herself together. Pause. She is looking away.*)

GIRL: What are you gonna do for Christmas?

JOHNNY: I don't know. What're you gonna do?

   (*She has covered her eyes.*)

   Are you all right?

   (*She sobs.*)

   What's the matter?

   (*She gets up quickly.*)

GIRL: Fuck off!

   (*She runs out of the room.* JOHNNY *stubs out his cigarette and*

gets up. There is a noise outside the room.)

The GIRL *is throwing Johnny's clothes and things out of the bathroom. When she has finished, she leans in the doorway in front of an opera poster (the Royal Opera: Attila).*

JOHNNY *comes out on to the landing and has a look. His stuff is strewn all down the stairs.*

JOHNNY: What's up, love? Was it something I said?

GIRL: I want you to go.

JOHNNY: Why?

GIRL: Can you go, please?!

JOHNNY: Is it 'cos I don't like dogs?

GIRL: Get out!!

JOHNNY: I don't quite follow, love.

GIRL: Just FUCK OFF!!

JOHNNY: Oh . . . I see. Well . . . perhaps I was jumpin' to conclusions, but I got the impression that I could kip down on the sofa or somethin'.

GIRL: GO!

JOHNNY: Go where?! 'Ave you got any suggestions? 'Cos it's like a fuckin' Eskimo's grave out there.

(*The* GIRL *suddenly starts chucking Johnny's things even further down the stairs.*)

Ey! Ey! (*Shouting*) All right, I'm goin'!! (*Screaming*) Ey!!

(*She stops and looks at him. After a moment, he charges down the stairs towards her. She backs up against the wall. They are now very close, face to face. There is a long, tense moment. Then, slowly,* JOHNNY *sinks to his knees and buries his face in her stomach. She goes to touch his hair, but doesn't.* JOHNNY *is unaware of this. He nestles his head slightly, then sits on the stairs at her feet. He starts putting on his shoes.*)

It's not easy, is it? D'you find that? Well . . . it just goes to show you that no matter 'ow many books you read, there's some things in this world that you never, ever, ever, ever, *ever* fuckin' understand. (*Pause. Then he does up his laces, gets up and sets off down the lower stairs. He stops and turns round.*) Oh . . . Thank you for the tea and the bath and the booze. And the beans. (*He picks up his things.*) An', er, listen, love . . . I hope that when you're tucked up tonight, all snug and warm underneath your tear-sodden fuckin' duvet in your ankle-length Emily Brontë windin'-sheet, that you spare a thought for me, with me head in a puddle of cold dog's piss. An' I hope that you dream about me. An' I hope that you wake up screamin'. (*He opens the door and goes into the lobby.*) An' I hope that all your fuckin' children are born blind, bow-legged, hare-lipped, homeless hunchbacks!!

(*He goes out through the front door, slamming it as he goes. The* GIRL *does not move.*)

At the same moment, LOUISE *and* SOPHIE *are sitting in a quiet pub, each with a pint glass.* SOPHIE *is smoking.*

LOUISE: 'Ave you ever 'ad an abortion?

SOPHIE: 'Ave you?

LOUISE: No. I thought I was pregnant once.

SOPHIE: Would you 'ave 'ad one?

LOUISE: Well, in the end it turned out I wasn't, and 'e left me anyway, so . . .

SOPHIE: I wanted to keep mine.

LOUISE: What happened?

SOPHIE: All my mates said I couldn't look after a baby. Too fuckin' right.

LOUISE: Did it make you feel shitty?

SOPHIE: It was a nightmare. I really loved 'im. 'E was a philosopher.

LOUISE: Where was this?

SOPHIE: Paris.

LOUISE: Paris?

SOPHIE: You should've seen the state of 'is girlfriend. 'Ad one when I was fifteen, an' all.

LOUISE: Oh, Jesus, Sophie!

SOPHIE: I think that one was worse for my mum, fuckin' drama she made out of it.

LOUISE: I could've been married by now, with a four-year-old.

SOPHIE: D'you wanna get married?

LOUISE: Dunno.

SOPHIE: Just 'cos you 'ave a kid with someone doesn't mean they're gonna stick around. My dad didn't. 'E couldn't fuckin' wait to get out.

LOUISE: Well, I don't know if I want to get married, but I wouldn't say no to a proper relationship.

SOPHIE: What is a proper relationship?

LOUISE: Livin' with someone 'oo talks to you after they've bonked you.

SOPHIE: I don't know what they want from you 'alf the time. What they start off likin' you for they end up hatin' you for. Don't like you if you're strong, don't like you if you're weak; hate you if you're clever, hate you if you're stupid. They don't know what they want. (*Pause.*) D'you think that bastard's fucked off yet?

LOUISE: Yeah, he musta done by now.

Much later that night. JOHNNY *is sitting, huddled in a doorway. Encrusted layers of posters surround him. A young* MAN *in a leather jacket arrives and starts putting up a large poster ('Therapy?'). * JOHNNY *gets up and watches him. He proceeds to put up a second copy of the same poster.*

JOHNNY: Is this a stick-up? Sorry – you must get that all the time, yeah?

MAN: Yeah.

JOHNNY: Just got it again. So is this your job, or a nice little hobby you've got for yourself? You're a lovely mover!

A minute or two later. The poster MAN *is closing up the back of his clapped-out old van. Then he gets in the front.* JOHNNY *opens the passenger door and leans in.*

JOHNNY: This your van, yeah?

MAN: Yeah.

JOHNNY: It's like, er, I dunno . . . top o' the range. Very nice. Are you goin' up the road?

MAN: D'you wanna lift?

JOHNNY: *(Laughs)* Is that all right with you, yeah? Cheers. *(He gets in.)* It's just, I've been walkin' round the streets all night, you know what I mean? These fuckin' feet are on their last legs, I'm tellin' you. *(The van moves off.)*

Inside the van. They speed along an empty main road.

JOHNNY: So, 'ow much d'you earn for doin' this?

MAN: It's none of your fuckin' business.

JOHNNY: I mean, is the pay as substantial as say, er, the wages of sin? You know what I mean? Are you with me?

A few minutes later. An illicit billboard site. The poster MAN *is preparing to hang a poster.*

JOHNNY: Listen, Captain, is it all right if I 'ave a go at doin' this, yeah? *(The* MAN *gives* JOHNNY *his long-handled brush.)* Oh! God love you! *(He dips the brush in the paste-bucket. The* MAN *gives him the folded poster.)* I mean, or does it take like thousands of years of like state-subsidized government training to do this clobber, yeah? *(He brushes paste on to an old poster on the hoarding.)* You've gotta slap on like copious quantities of the old industrial sputum there. *(He throws the brush on the ground.)* Beg your puddin'. *(The* MAN *picks the brush up.* JOHNNY *unfolds the new poster.)* It's a wonderful career opportunity for me – you know what I mean? (*He holds the poster in position.*) I'm gonna play the joker on this one. (*The top of the poster flops over* JOHNNY, *completely enveloping his head and shoulders.*)

MAN: Shift.

JOHNNY: It's all goin' very well . . . Ah! (*He punches the poster.*)

MAN: Shift out the fuckin' way, will you? (*He retrieves the poster.*)

JOHNNY: No, I like Laurel and Hardy, you know, although apparently they didn't get on in real life, you know – another illusion shattered.

(*The* MAN *hangs the poster.*)

Sorry about that, pal, it's just, I've 'ad a lot of bad experience with walls, you know, what with, er, talkin' to them and climbin' 'em, and me dad's driven me up a good few in 'is time, you know what I mean?

(*The* MAN *continues along the wall.* JOHNNY *follows.*)

But, er, I think I've got the secret. The saucy little secret, the solipsistic, sagacious little secret is just, you got – you just gotta (*head-butts wall*) bang your fuckin' head against them! (*He continues to head-butt the wall.*) Just . . . crack the old pate . . . Are you with me?!!

(*The* MAN *has now posted a small sign that just says 'Cancelled'. He moves on.* JOHNNY *follows. The* MAN *hangs three more 'Cancelled' signs,* JOHNNY *stopping each time he does so.*)

'Ave you got it? And that's it, that is the key to enlightenment, which is, which is it's, it's like that's why, that's why it's like such a potent motif of civilization – it's the wall. It's like the, the Great Wall of China, and, and, the Wall of Jericho and the Berlin Wall, and the Wailin' Wall. Now you see, the Jews . . . They've almost got it, an't they? What with the old rockin' and that, and, you know, just that six inches away and they'll be there, they'd 'ave won the fuckin' race, they'll be there, you with me? What is all this, anyway? What are you doin'? Cancel everythin'. In the beginnin' was the Word, and the word was 'CANCELLED'. D'you get like satisfaction out of this? D'you think you're makin' a contribution? You're like sort of publicly promulgatin' vacuities? Are you with me?

(*The* MAN *walks off briskly.*)

Fuckin' hell!!

(JOHNNY *follows.*)

Moments later. JOHNNY *follows the poster* MAN *to his van, which is parked on an empty main road.*

JOHNNY: Oh, that's it! Blank it all out! Blank it all out till you just atrophy and die of fuckin' indifference!

(*The man is closing his back doors.*)

Can I show you somethin', pal? You see that at the top of your legs? That's your arse and that's your fuckin' elbow! D'you wanna write it down, or s –

(*The* MAN *assaults* JOHNNY. *He knees him in the crutch and knocks him down. Then he kicks his arse very hard.*)

Aargh! Ow, fuck! Ow!

(*The* MAN *runs back to the van.*)

'Oos that supposed to be, me dad? You wanna watch that, mate – I've got a dicky sacrum 'ere.

(*The van door slams.*)

Shit!

(*The engine starts.* JOHNNY *starts crawling towards the van.*)

Er, can you, er, come back 'ere? Er, did I upset you? (*He gets up and staggers to the van. It moves off. He kicks it as it goes. He falls in the gutter.*) Ey! . . . (*Shouting*) You've got me bag!!!

(*He gets up and hollers after the vanishing van.*) You fuckin' tosser!! You f – (*He kicks and punches a metal waste-bin on a lamppost.*) Fuck!! (*A few cars pass. Then the street is empty again.* JOHNNY *continues to shout.*) Oh, listen!! Does anybody mind if I scream 'ere? Is it OK with you all? 'Cos I'd feel better for it – won't take long! (*He has drifted into the middle of the road.*) Aaargh!! Aaargh! Fuck. (*He drops to his knees. He crawls around in the road, twitching and coughing. A car swerves past him.*)

Later still. JOHNNY *is walking very slowly down an empty, narrow passage. A gang of youths appears. They soon catch up with* JOHNNY. *They stop and beat him up, quickly and thoroughly. Then they run off, shouting and screaming.* JOHNNY *lies in a heap on the ground, motionless.*

The house stands, tall and silent, in the dead of night.

Inside, LOUISE *and* SOPHIE *are asleep in Sandra's bed. Suddenly, the front-door bell rings. They wake up immediately.*

LOUISE: 'Oo's that?

> (LOUISE *puts on the light and sits up. Then she gets out of bed. She moves a chair from in front of Sandra's door, which she opens and goes through.*
> *She creeps downstairs, stopping once to listen for something on the upper floor.*
> *She opens the front door.* JOHNNY *falls in, head-first. He is seriously bruised and bleeding.*)

Oh, Jesus!

> (*Now she is helping* JOHNNY *as he staggers upstairs, grunting and groaning.*)

What's been happenin' to you? Will you shut up, for God's sake?

> (*At the first landing, he falls on the floor.* LOUISE *touches his bruised face.*)

JOHNNY: Ow!

LOUISE: (*Whispering*) I'm sorry, I'm sorry, I'm sorry.

JOHNNY: Just give us a fag.

> (*She reaches for one.*)

Fuckin' comedian.

> (*She puts a cigarette in his mouth, but he sits up, sobbing, and it falls out.*)

It's not my fault.

LOUISE: What's not your fault?

> (*He staggers up the next half-flight of stairs.*)

Where are you goin'?

JOHNNY: I just wanna go to bed.

LOUISE: Be quiet! (*She follows him.*)

JOHNNY: I fuckin' walked 'ere.

LOUISE: From where?

> (*He falls against the wall on the half-landing.* SOPHIE *comes out on to the top landing above.*)

SOPHIE: Johnny . . .

JOHNNY: Um . . . I'm . . . I'm gonna be sick.

> (LOUISE *runs back downstairs.* JOHNNY, *hopping on one leg, staggers up to Sophie's landing.* LOUISE *rushes back with a small plastic bowl.* JOHNNY *collapses at Sophie's feet.* LOUISE *arrives.* JOHNNY *is gasping heavily.*)

SOPHIE: Fuckin' 'ell! What's 'appened to 'im?

LOUISE: I dunno.

SOPHIE: Johnny . . . are you all right, Johnny? (*She touches him.*)

JOHNNY: Get off!!

LOUISE/SOPHIE: Sssh!!

> (*They both look round.*)

SOPHIE: Is 'e still 'ere?

LOUISE: I dunno . . .

> (*Very gingerly, they creep to Sophie's room and peer round the door.* JEREMY *is asleep on the bed, still undressed, and clutching the champagne bottle and an empty glass. He is snoring. The girls withdraw, closing the door.*
> *Back on the landing, they contemplate* JOHNNY. *They whisper.*)
> Right, we'd better get 'im into bed.

SOPHIE: Yeah.

LOUISE: You take that end, I'll take this end. (*She moves towards Johnny's head.*)

SOPHIE: OK, don't push me, right?

LOUISE: I'm not pushin' you!

> (*They bend down.*)
> Careful, that's 'is bad leg.

SOPHIE: Well, what d'you want me to do?

LOUISE: After three. One, two, three.

> (*They begin to lift him.*)

JOHNNY: (*Crying*)I wanna go! I wanna go!!

> (JOHNNY *now has a fit. But this is confusion, not anger. He kicks, screams, bangs the wall and floor, and rolls around. An ironing board falls on him and the girls pull it off. He mumbles, cries and shouts. Perhaps he refers to his mother at one point, but for the most part his utterances are incomprehensible.*
> *After a while,* JEREMY *emerges from Sophie's room and watches* JOHNNY *alongside the horrified girls.*
> *Eventually, the thrashing around subsides.* JOHNNY *is out of breath. He suddenly notices* JEREMY. *A look of recognition and terror creeps into his eyes. He is very distressed. He speaks to* JEREMY.)
> I know. I know, you told me. I'm . . . I'm not here yet. I'm still wet.
> (*Tears well in Louise's eyes.*)

What did she mean? Why not me brother? (*Crying*) Will it be quiet now? (*He reaches for Jeremy's hand.*) Are we goin'? (*As he touches him,* JEREMY *recoils and, like an electric shock, they all four jump.*)

Fuck!

(JOHNNY *is now lying in the doorway to Sandra's room. He is still crying a bit and is obviously in pain. Pause. They all watch him.*)

JEREMY: Who's this?

LOUISE: It's all right, 'e's a friend of mine.

JEREMY: What extraordinary friends you have. He's only got one sock on.

SOPHIE: Shut up!

JEREMY: You seem a bit tense, Sophie. Would you like a massage?

JOHNNY: Are you the doctor?

JEREMY: Pardon?

JOHNNY: Is he the doctor?

JEREMY: You're rather disgusting, aren't you?

(SOPHIE *touches Louise's arm gently.*)

You're not crying, are you, Louise?

SOPHIE: Oh, listen, when are you gonna fuck off?! This 'as got nothin' to do with you, right?

(JEREMY *grabs hold of* SOPHIE *and tries to kiss her.* LOUISE *drops to the floor, with her hands protecting her head.*)

No! No!

(SOPHIE *screams.* JEREMY *lets her go.*)

SOPHIE: Leave me alone! (*She squats down with* LOUISE.)

JOHNNY: Fuckin' 'ell, me leg! You don't know.

JEREMY: Aren't people pathetic? Right. I'm going to beddy-byes. (*He goes into Sophie's room and reappears immediately.*)

If anyone wishes to join me, I'll be under the duvet. (*He goes to bed.* SOPHIE *touches* LOUISE. LOUISE *wipes her eyes. They whisper.*)

SOPHIE: Are you all right?

LOUISE: Yeah. Are you?

SOPHIE: Yeah. Come on, I'll give you a hand.

JOHNNY: I'm all right, I walked 'ere.

(*He staggers across Sandra's room and onto her bed, gasping.*)

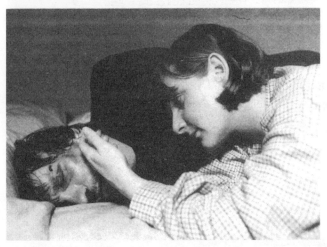

LOUISE *follows. She lies next to him. He is on his side, exhausted.*
She is on her tummy, propping herself up on her arms.)

JOHNNY: Is it 'ere?

LOUISE: Yeah.

JOHNNY: 'Oos's that?

LOUISE: Clancy.

JOHNNY: I thought so. I used to know you, didn't I?

LOUISE: Yeah.

(JOHNNY *begins to sing.* LOUISE *joins in. She sings consistently,*
but JOHNNY *comes and goes.*)

JOHNNY/LOUISE: Take me back to Manchester when it's raining.

I want to wet me feet in Albert Square.

I'm all agog

For a good, thick fog.

I don't like the sun,

I like it raining cats and dogs!

I want to smell the odours of the Irwell.

I want to feel the soot get in me 'air.

Oh, I don't want to roam.

I want to get back 'ome

To rainy

Manchester . . .

JOHNNY: I've got an 'ard-on.

(LOUISE *smiles and touches his cheek with the back of her hand.*
SOPHIE, *sucking her fingers in the corner of the room, turns to the*
wall.)

Early next morning. Grey light. A black taxi pulls up outside the
house. SANDRA *gets out, wearing her jacket and shorts, her sandals*
and her white socks, with her straw safari hat on her back. She pays
the driver and climbs the steps with her luggage.

She clambers all the way to the top of the house and proceeds to enter
her room, the door of which is open. She stops in the doorway. Three
people are asleep in her bed.

SANDRA: What's . . .? (*She drops the luggage and advances towards*
the culprits.) What are you . . .? This is . . . It's disgusting!

(LOUISE *sits up with a jolt, instantly awake.*)

Nobody . . . in my . . . Who's 'e? You've got your boots on!

79

She's . . . And what's this doing? (*She picks up her uniform from the floor.*) This is something that I can't . . . I don't . . . it's not . . . I just . . . don't need all this . . . palaver. (*She has left the room and gone downstairs.*)

LOUISE: Oh, shit!

(LOUISE *races into her room, closing the door behind her.* SANDRA *comes back upstairs, carrying Jeremy's jacket.*)

SANDRA: OK, who's Jeremy?

(LOUISE *comes out of her room, putting on her tights.*)
Who's Jeremy?

LOUISE: What d'you mean?

(JEREMY *appears from Sophie's room, still wearing only his underpants.*)

JEREMY: Sandra! What a nice surprise!

SANDRA: What are you doing here?

JEREMY: How was Zimbabwe?

SANDRA: Shift! (*She pushes* JEREMY *aside and enters Sophie's room.*)

JEREMY: Morning, Louise.

(*He giggles and disappears.* SANDRA *comes out of Sophie's room.*)

SANDRA: Where's Jeremy? (*She goes into Louise's room.*)

LOUISE: 'Oo's Jeremy?

(SANDRA *comes out of Louise's room.*)

SANDRA: These are Jeremy's.

(*She holds up a wallet.* JEREMY *reappears at the top of the stairs.*)

LOUISE: That's Sebastian's.

SANDRA: No, look. (*She takes out some credit cards.*) Jeremy Smart; Jeremy Smart; Jeremy G. Smart.

LOUISE: Well, I've never 'eard of him.

(JEREMY *sniggers.*)

SANDRA: Sebastian. Who – ? (*She confronts him.*) Are you Jeremy G. Smart? Are you?

(*She follows him downstairs.* LOUISE *rushes back to Sandra's bed.*)

LOUISE: Johnny! Johnny . . . Wake up.

SOPHIE: (*Sitting up*) Just leave 'im.

LOUISE: Oh, for fuck's sake, Sophie, Sandra's back.

SOPHIE: What day is it?

LOUISE: It's Friday.

80

SOPHIE: Fuck this.

LOUISE: Look at 'is eye.

SOPHIE: Christ.

LOUISE: Well, 'e can lie down in my room – oh, God! (*She inspects his bruised ankle.*)

SOPHIE: What are you doin'? 'E's not 'arming anyone.

LOUISE: 'Ave you seen the state of 'er? Johnny . . .

SOPHIE: I'm here, Johnny.

(*Enter* JEREMY *carrying his jacket, and* SANDRA, *with his trousers.*)

JEREMY: Morning, everyone! (*He goes to the bedside table to get his watch.*)

SANDRA: I would actually like to have some kind of explanation for all this, because –

JEREMY: Having fun?

SANDRA: Can you put these on, please?

JEREMY: Sophie and I had a fuck on your bed yesterday afternoon, Sandra.

SOPHIE: Oh, God!

SANDRA: You are just –

JEREMY: She was very good, I must say.

SANDRA: – filth!

JEREMY: Not as good as you, though.

SANDRA: You lying . . . nastiness! (*She throws the trousers at him.*)

JEREMY: We must do it again sometime.

(*He sniggers and leaves the room.* SANDRA *follows him out, but stops in the doorway and turns to* LOUISE *and* SOPHIE.)

SANDRA: Will you . . .? How can you . . .? Everything! (*She goes.*)

SOPHIE: I can't cope with this.

(LOUISE *closes her eyes.* SANDRA *and* JEREMY *can be heard downstairs.*)

SANDRA: Right, you've got five minutes.

JEREMY: Pardon?

SANDRA: Five minutes to get your things on and get the hell –

JEREMY: I shouldn't worry about things, if I were you.

A few minutes later. In the kitchen. SANDRA *is busily filling a black bin-liner with Louise's and Sophie's garbage.* JEREMY, *now wearing his shirt, stands watching her.*

81

JEREMY: I'd forgotten what a beautiful bottom you've got, Sandra.

SANDRA: Two minutes.

(JEREMY *sniggers and leaves.* LOUISE, *now dressed, passes him in the doorway.*)

JEREMY: (*To* LOUISE) Marvellous tits.

(*He goes.* LOUISE *hovers for a moment, but lets it go. She joins* SANDRA.)

LOUISE: Listen, Sandra. I'm really sorry. We weren't expectin' you back.

(SANDRA *stops working.*)

SANDRA: I fail to . . . why . . . it's a pigsty . . . it's . . .

LOUISE: I know – it just got out of 'and.

SANDRA: Obviously. And what's all that? (*She points in the direction of upstairs.*)

LOUISE: 'E's a friend o' mine – Look, can I make you a cup o' tea?

SANDRA: I don't want tea . . . I don't want . . . I just want . . . My journey was –

LOUISE: He's not very well!

(SANDRA *resumes work.*)

SANDRA: What's the matter with 'im?

LOUISE: 'E's got a lump on 'is face the size of a boiled egg an' 'e won't wake up.

(SANDRA *stops working again. She looks at* LOUISE, *throws down the bin-liner and marches out of the kitchen.* LOUISE *inspects a cornflakes packet, throws it away, and proceeds to fill the kettle.*)

Minutes later. Up in her bedroom, SANDRA *is standing surveying* JOHNNY, *who is still asleep, and* SOPHIE, *who is sitting up in bed.*

SANDRA: Did he do this?

SOPHIE: 'Oo?

SANDRA: Sebastian – Jeremy?

SOPHIE: You never warned me about 'im, did you?

SANDRA: What are you talking about?

SOPHIE: Fuckin' lettin' 'imself in with the keys! Bastard!

(SANDRA *goes to the end of the bed.*)

SANDRA: I don't . . . Right. Let's get this shoe off. (*She removes*

Johnny's shoe, revealing his bruised ankle, which we now see in close-up: it is pretty bad.)

Meanwhile, in the kitchen, LOUISE *is wiping up a mug.* JEREMY *wanders in. He is now wearing his trousers.*

JEREMY: Have you ever had smoked salmon after making love, Louise?

LOUISE: I don't like smoked salmon.

JEREMY: I think you should try it. It's rather wonderful.

LOUISE: Will you undo your flies, Sebastian?

JEREMY: Would you like me to?

(LOUISE *puts down the mug and tea-towel, turns to face* JEREMY *and nods.*)

LOUISE: Honest.

(*Without taking his eyes off* LOUISE, JEREMY *moves towards her a little. He unzips his flies.* LOUISE *returns his smug, expectant smile with a confident, challenging air. Then she lowers her eyes and moves close to him with a more subordinate, dutiful, almost concubine demeanour. A moment passes. Then she wheels round, seizes a large kitchen knife from the draining board and thrusts it at* JEREMY, *who recoils with a look of horror.*)

Or d'you not want me to slice your prick off and shove it up your arse?

(*They face each other. She looks as though she means business. For a moment, he is stuck. Then he sniggers, rather mirthlessly and unconvincingly, and, turning his back on her, he slinks towards the door.*)

Maggot dick! (*She watches him leave the room. Then she throws down the knife and leans over the sink in disgust.*)

A little later, back in Sandra's room. LOUISE *stands watching as* SANDRA *attends to Johnny's foot.* JOHNNY *is now awake.* SOPHIE *is still sitting up in the bed.*

SANDRA: (*To* SOPHIE) Could you pass me that pillow, please?

SOPHIE: I can't move, Sandra.

(LOUISE *passes it.*)

LOUISE: 'Ere you go.

SANDRA: You are worse than useless.

(SANDRA *places the pillow under Johnny's foot. He groans.*)

LOUISE: Ooh, are y'all right? You don't think it's broken, do you?

SANDRA: No, 'e can move it. You can do that, can't you? (*She waggles her hand from the wrist.*)

JOHNNY: Why would I want to do that?

(*He repeats the hand gesture.* SOPHIE *is about to light a cigarette.*)

SANDRA: Don't even . . . not in my room, Sophie.

(SOPHIE *doesn't light it.*)

SOPHIE: I need a fag.

SANDRA: I don't care . . . cop hold o' that.

(*She gives* SOPHIE *a small plastic container from a medical tray beside her.*)

SOPHIE: Just don't start, right?

(*Holding a cotton-wool swab with a pair of tweezers,* SANDRA *dabs antiseptic on Johnny's ankle, then drops the swab in the container held by* SOPHIE.)

SANDRA: It really is beyond me the way you girls choose to live your lives. My mind just . . . boggles.

LOUISE: 'E's gone back to sleep.

(SANDRA *prepares a fresh swab. A door slams. The girls all look round.*)

Was that the front door?

SOPHIE: 'E's gone.
SANDRA: Thank God. (*She dabs Johnny's ankle.*)

Below, in the street, Jeremy gets into his car and drives off.

A little later. Supported by SANDRA, *who has his arm round her shoulders,* JOHNNY *is hobbling downstairs. His ankle is now neatly bandaged.* LOUISE *and* SOPHIE *follow.*
LOUISE: Go slowly, Johnny.
SANDRA: Now, what you two must do is take this one to Casualty and make sure he gets himself looked at, 'fore he goes home.
JOHNNY: I'm gonna be sick.
SANDRA: Are you?
LOUISE: Get 'im to the bathroom!
    (*She goes towards the kitchen.* SOPHIE *sinks on to the stairs. We hold on her.*)
SANDRA: (*Out of vision*) All right! All right! Let's not . . . just a minute. (*From the bathroom.*) That's it. Take it steady.
    (LOUISE *rushes past* SOPHIE.)
LOUISE: Here y'are.

A few minutes later, in the bathroom. JOHNNY *is on the floor, leaning over the open lavatory bowl.* LOUISE *squats beside him, holding a blue face-flannel.*
JOHNNY: It's in me tash.
    (LOUISE *wipes his moustache.*)
LOUISE: You wanna gerrit cut. It's in your mouth. (*She gets up to rinse the flannel.*) 'Ave you 'ad a bath lately?
JOHNNY: Yeah, I 'ad one yesterday.
LOUISE: As if!
JOHNNY: I did!
    (SOPHIE *is standing by the door, holding a cigarette.*)
SOPHIE: Where've you been, Johnny?
JOHNNY: Down the Via Dolorosa. Don't be nosy.
    (SOPHIE *sits on the edge of the bath.* SANDRA *bustles past the open door.* LOUISE *has sat on the other end of the bath, by the sink.*)
    Are you not goin' to work?
LOUISE: I'm late.
    (SANDRA *passes in the other direction, with the vacuum cleaner.*)

JOHNNY: Oh, you'll get the sack.

LOUISE: Yeah.

JOHNNY: It's all right – you can put all your troubles in it. 'Ey, I lost me bag.

LOUISE: Yeah, I noticed. Where is it?

JOHNNY: I don't know. It's lost.

LOUISE: Any valuables?

JOHNNY: Yeah, it's got me collection of famous retired glove-puppets in there.

(LOUISE *smiles*.)

That's it – all gone.

SOPHIE: Did you get it nicked?

(JOHNNY *looks at* SOPHIE.)

JOHNNY: Would you put that out?

(SOPHIE *freezes*. JOHNNY *looks at* LOUISE. LOUISE *looks from* JOHNNY *to* SOPHIE. SOPHIE *looks at her cigarette*. LOUISE *holds out her hand*. SOPHIE *gives her the cigarette*. LOUISE *puts it out under the tap and throws it away. Throughout this, the vacuum cleaner can be heard in the living room*.)

LOUISE: I 'an't cleaned me teeth yet.

(*She picks up her toothbrush*. JOHNNY *has sat back against the towel-rail*.)

JOHNNY: Could you not just put 'em in a glass or somethin', no?

(LOUISE *perches on the bath and brushes her teeth*. JOHNNY *closes the lavatory. There is plainly a rapport between them*. SOPHIE *looks desperately from* JOHNNY *to* LOUISE. LOUISE *glances back at* SOPHIE, *then gets up to rinse out her mouth at the sink. She is now standing with her back to* JOHNNY. *He touches her garment, the same trouser-skirt that* JEREMY *fingered yesterday*.)

I remember when you bought these shorts. I warned you about 'em then.

LOUISE: Yeah . . . well . . . (*She swills her mouth, spits out the water and sits on the bath*.) I only got 'em to piss you off.

JOHNNY: Mission accomplished.

(SANDRA *appears at the door*.)

SANDRA: Is he all right?

LOUISE: Yeah.

(SANDRA *leaves*.)

JOHNNY: What is this, a spectator sport or something? The 100-metre vomit.

(SOPHIE *smiles sadly.* LOUISE *looks at her.*)

LOUISE: Sophie, d'you mind if I 'ave a word with Johnny on me own?

(*Pause.*)

SOPHIE: D'you want a word with Louise on your own?

JOHNNY: Are you bein' sarcastic?

SOPHIE: No.

JOHNNY: Well, do as you're told.

(LOUISE *looks at the floor.*)

SOPHIE: (*Quietly*) Right . . .

(*She gets up slowly. Just as she has gone through the door,* SANDRA *appears again, clutching a wad of paper money.*)

SANDRA: Whose is all this money? Three hundred and eighty pounds, it really oughtn't to be left lying waiting for . . .

(*She drifts back to the living room. Pause.* LOUISE *gets up and closes the door.* SOPHIE *is now sitting on the stairs outside the bathroom.* LOUISE *stands for a moment by the door, on which there is another anatomical diagram.*)

JOHNNY: Whose is all that?

LOUISE: Dunno. (*She sits on the floor, facing* JOHNNY.) Who's been playin' ping-pong with your face?

JOHNNY: The sky fell in on me. A cloud caught me across the cheek.

LOUISE: So, why did you come to London?

JOHNNY: I come to run in the Marathon.

LOUISE: Will you give me a straight answer, please?

JOHNNY: Well, I 'ad to get out of Manchester 'cos I was gonna get a beatin'. And I come down 'ere and, er . . . get a beatin'.

LOUISE: Were you askin' for it?

JOHNNY: No. I wasn't. They just come out of nowhere.

LOUISE: Honest?

JOHNNY: Yeah.

(*Pause.*)

So what are you gonna do?

LOUISE: What are *you* gonna do?

JOHNNY: What are *you* gonna do?

LOUISE: Dunno. Might go 'ome for the weekend.

JOHNNY: Well, there's no place like it.

LOUISE: Might not come back. Are you goin' back?

(*He rubs her bottom gently with his bare foot [the good one]*.)

JOHNNY: Is that nice?

LOUISE: Yeah.

JOHNNY: I'm puttin' the fun back in 'fundament'.

LOUISE: Are yer?

JOHNNY: Well, I'll 'ave to go back sometime, won't I?

LOUISE: And what about us?

JOHNNY: What about us?

(*Pause.*)

LOUISE: Do you hate me?

JOHNNY: Fuck off!

(*Pause.*)

My mam was seven years younger than you when she 'ad me.

LOUISE: Don't.

JOHNNY: What?

LOUISE: Just . . .

JOHNNY: Well, she was! (*Chortles a bit.*) I'm full o' shit, aren't I?

LOUISE: Sometimes.

JOHNNY: Yeah, well, it's all right. I've 'ad it all kicked out of me now.

LOUISE: Oh? Good.

JOHNNY: What if God just put us 'ere for his own entertainment? That's all we are. Just somethin' for 'im to 'ave a bit of a laugh at. Could be, coun'n't it? If you think about it. (*He has picked up a 'Toilet Duck'.*) Give us your right 'and.

(*She holds it out, palm-down.*)

Other way up.

(*She turns it palm-up. Using the 'Toilet Duck' as the 'Dadaist Nun', JOHNNY repeats Brian's security procedure on the palm of Louise's hand, rendering the electronic-bleep sound vocally. He repeats all this on her forehead. She laughs.*)

LOUISE: What's that?

JOHNNY: That's funny to me.

LOUISE: You're daft, you.

JOHNNY: It's, er, toilet humour.

LOUISE: Will you give me a cuddle, Johnny?

JOHNNY: Yeah.

A few minutes later. SOPHIE *is sobbing her heart out on the stairs. In the bathroom,* LOUISE *snuggles up to* JOHNNY, *who has his arm round her. They can hear* SOPHIE.

A bit later. LOUISE *is alone in her room, reflecting.* SANDRA *can just be heard downstairs, trying to talk to* SOPHIE, *who is still wailing.*

A little later still. The living room. JOHNNY *is resting on the sofa.* SOPHIE *is still crying. She is kneeling beside him, but behind the sofa.* SANDRA *bustles in with a water-spray and proceeds to refresh her plants.*

SANDRA: If no one tells me what's going on, then how am I supposed –

SOPHIE: I don't understand, Johnny!

JOHNNY: 'Ow was Zambia?

SANDRA: It was Zimbabwe! I went to Zimbabwe with my wanker boyfriend, my ex –

SOPHIE: What did I do wrong?

JOHNNY: Did you see any big animals?

SANDRA: Yes! We saw elephants and rhinos and zebras and lions and vultures . . .

JOHNNY: Did you see any monkeys?

SANDRA: We saw many monkeys.

JOHNNY: And were they cheeky?
   (SOPHIE *strokes his hair.*)
   Oh, it's not good for me, is it, all this, in my condition?
   (SOPHIE'*s bawling continues.*)

SANDRA: Well, yes, no, yes . . . it's not good for me. It's not good for you. It's not good for any of us, it's utterly . . . (*She scuttles out.*)

SOPHIE: Oh, excuse me for living!! (*Sobbing*) Is, is this it, Johnny? Is it?

JOHNNY: Is what it?

SOPHIE: (*In pain*) Oh, I can't bear it! (*She shakes the sofa, then disappears down behind it.*) Right! I'm off! (*She gets up and walks away.*)

JOHNNY: Off your trolley.
   (SOPHIE *comes back and smacks him hard around the head. He holds up his hands in self-defence.*)

SOPHIE: Oh, don't fuckin' take the piss out of me, you bastard!!

You don't know!
(She leaves as SANDRA *returns.)*

SANDRA: All I want . . . Nobody has any . . . *(She leaves.)*
(From outside) Can you just please try and . . .

SOPHIE: *(Off)* I've 'ad enough.

SANDRA: *(Off)* This is a nightmare!
*(*JOHNNY *is left alone, nursing his head.)*

Shortly after this. On the steps of the house. The front door opens.
SOPHIE *rushes out, still crying. She is wearing her hat and coat, and is
carrying a holdall and a large chromium-plated letter 'S'.* SANDRA
and LOUISE *follow her out.*

SANDRA: Sophie, if you could just try and pull yourself together.

LOUISE: Where are you goin'?

SOPHIE: I don't know.

SANDRA: Why don't you come in and have a lie-down?

SOPHIE: I don't care!

LOUISE: Sophie!

SOPHIE: 'Ere's the keys! *(She offers them to* SANDRA.)

SANDRA: I don't want the keys! *(She holds up her hands.)*

SOPHIE: Well, I don't fuckin' wan' 'em! *(She throws them on the
step.)*

SANDRA: *(Shouting)* I'm not a social worker!
(She goes indoors. Still sobbing desperately, SOPHIE *runs down
the steps with her possessions.* LOUISE *follows.)*

LOUISE: Look, Sophie . . . don't be fuckin' stupid!

SOPHIE: What's the point, Louise? *(She sets off down the road.)*

LOUISE: Sophie!
*(*SOPHIE *turns for a moment.)*

SOPHIE: I'm sorry!
*(And, sobbing uncontrollably, off she goes. At the end of the
street, she disappears round the corner.* LOUISE *watches her go.
Then she walks thoughtfully back up the steps, goes into the house
and closes the front door.)*

Moments later, in the living room. JOHNNY *is lying on the sofa with
the blue flannel on his face.* LOUISE *is kneeling in front of him.*

LOUISE: *(Quietly)* Johnny. *(She removes the flannel.)* Are you
all right?

JOHNNY: Mm?

LOUISE: I'm goin'.

JOHNNY: Where?

LOUISE: Work. To 'and me notice in. Then I'm comin' back 'ere,
I'm packin' me bags and I'm goin' 'ome. D'you wanna come?

JOHNNY: Today?

LOUISE: Yeah.

JOHNNY: Are you serious?

LOUISE: Yeah.

JOHNNY: 'Ow?

LOUISE: Bus.

  (*Pause.*)

JOHNNY: Well, 'ave you got enough dough?

LOUISE: Yeah.

JOHNNY: 'Cos I've got nothin'.

LOUISE: I know. (*Pause.*) D'you think you can make it?

JOHNNY: Don't know.

LOUISE: Well, if you don't, we can stay 'ere till tomorrow. (*She
kisses him on the mouth, properly, tenderly.*) See you later.

JOHNNY: Er, can you leave us a few fags for cancer research?

  (SANDRA *comes in, holding Johnny's shoes.*)

SANDRA: Here are your . . .

(*She puts them down.* JOHNNY *is taking the cigarettes from* LOUISE.)

I was actually hoping that the air could . . . (*She picks up the wad of money.*) What are we gonna do about all this . . .

(LOUISE *joins her at the sideboard.*)

LOUISE: I dunno, Sandra. Look, I'll see you in a couple of hours.

SANDRA: Fine.

JOHNNY: Er, you will come back?

(LOUISE *stops in the doorway.*)

LOUISE: Yeah, course I will.

SANDRA: Because I need . . .

LOUISE: You'll be all right, won't you?

JOHNNY: (*To* SANDRA) Will I be all right, love?

SANDRA: I'm gonna get the bath cleaned.

(*She leaves.* JOHNNY *and* LOUISE *look at each other for a while. Then, with a twinkle in her eye,* LOUISE *turns and leaves.* JOHNNY *listens as she goes down the stairs and out of the house.*)

A few minutes later. JOHNNY *is sitting on the sofa, smoking a cigarette.*

SANDRA *comes in with an ashtray.*

SANDRA: You all know what it does to you and yet you still insist on doing it, so . . . do it. Smoke yourself to . . .

(JOHNNY *takes the ashtray.*)

JOHNNY: Well, birds do it, bees do it.

SANDRA: . . . high heaven. (*She puts a cushion on a low table in front of* JOHNNY.)

JOHNNY: Can you tell me something, love? Is it true that, er, some babies are born covered in fur?

SANDRA: Up!

(JOHNNY *raises his foot with a little difficulty.* SANDRA *places it on the cushion.*)

Thank you. (*She puts a tea-towel on the radiator.*)

JOHNNY: And you know at birth, when you cut the umbilical cord? What would 'appen if, if, um . . . well, if it was never cut?

(SANDRA *reverses a decorative fire-screen, which has been facing the wall.*)

SANDRA: I don't need this – I just . . .

JOHNNY: Well, it would be embarrassin', wouldn't it? Specially at my age.

SANDRA: Why do you feel the need . . . to take the piss?

JOHNNY: I'm not takin' the piss. It's nice that (*the firescreen*) – where's it from?

SANDRA: I don't know, it's something my dad . . .
(*They look at it.*)

JOHNNY: Now you see, Sophie just turned that to the wall. She's got this kind of, er, irritatin' proclivity for negation – I suppose she thinks it's progressive or somethin'.

SANDRA: What is your problem?

JOHNNY: Nothing. What's your problem?

SANDRA: All these silly questions and . . .

JOHNNY: Well, look, I've never met a nurse before, and I'm just interested in, er . . . well, in life. I mean, d'you think it's worth savin'?

SANDRA: Of course I do. But there is a time and a place, and actually this isn't the time or . . .

JOHNNY: The place?

SANDRA: No. And this . . . is where I . . .

JOHNNY: Live?

SANDRA: Yes. And I'm not feeling very . . .

JOHNNY: Sexy.

SANDRA: Comfortable, actually. I'm not feeling very comfortable.

JOHNNY: Well, make yourself comfortable, love. Or slip into something more (*Mouths 'comfortable'.*)

SANDRA: My bath! Hot toast . . . hot milk . . . hot-water bottle . . . bed, sleep.

JOHNNY: D'you like me?

SANDRA: I don't know you, so . . .

JOHNNY: D'you find me attractive?
(SANDRA *is speechless.*)
Well, listen, love, it's like this. I find you attractive. Very attractive.

SANDRA: Enough. I've had enough. It comes at me from all angles. You all of you just . . . it's the tin lid . . . When . . . how . . . will . . . the world . . . ever . . .

JOHNNY: End.

SANDRA: Yes!
(*She looks at him for a moment in great agitation. Then she*

94

walks out of the room. JOHNNY *takes a slow drag on his cigarette and looks out of the window.)*

Shortly after this, SANDRA *is soaking up to her neck in a bathful of suds. Her eyes are closed. She sighs contentedly.*

At the same moment, in the living room, JOHNNY *reaches for his shoes and puts them on.*

Then he picks up the money, checks it briefly and stuffs it into his pocket.

Moments later, he comes out of the house. He hops down the steps and through the gate. Then he inches along a wall. For a moment he hangs on to a post.

Then he hobbles slowly down the middle of the very long road. Cars are parked on both sides. As he progresses, the receding house looms behind him. Once, he looks over his shoulder for a second. He carries on. A couple of people cross the road in the distance behind him.

JOHNNY *keeps going . . .*
We cut to black.